On Living with a Concern
for Gospel Ministry

BY

BRIAN DRAYTON

Quaker Press

OF FRIENDS GENERAL CONFERENCE
PHILADELPHIA, PA

Published in cooperation with
Mosher Book and Tract Fund of New England Yearly Meeting.

ISBN-10: 1-888305-38-X
ISBN-13: 978-1-888305-38-8

Library of Congress Cataloging-in-Publication Data
  Drayton, Brian.
    On living with a concern for gospel ministry / by Brian Drayton.
    p. cm.
  Includes bibliographical references.
  ISBN-13: 978-1-888305-38-8
  ISBN-10: 1-888305-38-X
  1. Pastoral theology—Society of Friends.   I. Title.
  BX7745.D73 2005
  253–dc22   2005029473

Cover art: *An Expression of Light* (watercolor) by Darcy Drayton

Book design and composition by David Budmen

For further information about this publication
and other Quaker resources, please contact:

Friends General Conference
1216 Arch Street, 2B
Philadelphia, PA 19107
215-561-1700
Or find us at www.fgcquaker.org

To order this or other publications call 800-966-4556,
e-mail bookstore@fgcquaker.org or you can order from us on the web at
www.quakerbooks.org.

Contents

iii

On Living with a Concern for Gospel Ministry

Contents

Foreword

My first contact with Brian Drayton was at New England Yearly Meeting in 1983 when Bill Taber gave a series of Bible half hours on "The Prophets and the Quaker Connection." Out of their meeting at that time Bill and Brian developed an ongoing relationship around their common interest in the vocal ministry and their commitment to faithfulness in nurturing and living out a call to ministry. Bill sought Brian's collaboration over a period of years in leading a series of five Pendle Hill weekends on traveling in the ministry; they led a workshop on the same topic at a Friends General Conference Gathering. In this way Bill Taber nurtured and encouraged the gift of ministry and of interpretation of Quaker spirituality that he saw in Brian.

In the fall of 2004 Bill and I had the opportunity to read Brian's draft of *On Living with a Concern for Gospel Ministry* and encourage him in this project. We had long felt that Brian's voice with his interpretation of Quaker spirituality deserves to be heard widely among Friends. Bill would join me in enthusiastically recommending this work to Friends across the spectrum of our theology and practice.

For those who are puzzled or put off by Brian's up-front use of the traditional term "gospel ministry" it may be helpful to be introduced at once to his definition of the term as given in the introduction. "Gospel ministry is service whose goal is to encourage, support, push, or invite people to seek and respond to the guidance, teaching and activity of that Light and Life at work in all, right now."

Brian provides a thorough treatment of all aspects and ramifications of the vocal ministry in the setting of unprogrammed or waiting worship among Friends. He is sensitive to the topic in its many subtle nuances. His handling of the subject will be of value equally to persons quite unfamiliar with the history and experience of the vocal ministry in the Religious Society of Friends, and to those who come with familiarity with and reverence for that tradition. Such breadth of reach is achieved by Brian's remarkable gift for linking the spirit and language of early Friends with that of the current period in a way that makes our history available to nourish us in the present time.

But this work is relevant not only to those living with a concern for the ministry. Many of the specifics are applicable to Friends under the weight of other concerns. It will be of service to those many Friends who over time live with any "concern" in the Quaker sense of the term-whether it be for peace, for the environment, for social justice. It may be especially helpful for Friends who carry a concern for nurturing the spiritual life of individuals and of the meeting as a whole in ways that do not often include the spoken ministry in meeting for worship.

Brian's work will be valuable as well to any Friend for a variety of reasons. It gives valuable instruction in the life of devotion and prayer-a clarification of the process rarely seen in Friends writings. It provides an accessible argument for the need for "deep exploration of Quakerism's resources as a major spiritual path." It gets to the inside of the process of the work of God in the heart, describing it in a way that links his own experience and that of other Friends today to generations of earlier Quaker experience. The process that Brian throws light on is in fact the inward work of Christ in the heart, the core of the Quaker understanding of Christianity. Indeed I find here a comprehensive, spiritually grounded understanding of Quakerism, especially unprogrammed Quakerism today and the many challenges it faces, relating them to a discussion of the ministry.

This work grows out of a life of faith, rooted and grounded in Brian's own ongoing experiment with applied faith in his own life. Out of personal experience he presents a deep searching of the interior life in a way that is rare in contemporary Quaker writing. It is comparable in its inward reach to the reflections on their spiritual condition of the early Quaker journalists while being presented in a language more accessible to modern readers. It offers the grace and helpfulness of a language to describe the interior life, what Bill Taber called the inward landscape, that is sensitive, perceptive, acute, with a kind of precision that comes from knowledge born of experience.

Brian Drayton has provided Friends with a thoughtful, faithful explication of authentic Quaker spirituality. I look forward to referring to his words in the future to stimulate my own attentiveness to the Inward Guide and to call me to faithfulness. As reading this text has been serviceable to me, I believe it can be to many Friends.

— FRAN TABER
OCTOBER 2005

Acknowledgements

It is a pleasure to remember the friends who have helped me along the way with this book. First and foremost, Darcy Drayton, spouse and spiritual friend whose love, intelligence, and witness have been nourishing and instructive. Then dear friends from Fresh Pond Meeting who read and critiqued the book, and have been companions in much of my learning: Bruce Neumann, Will and Lynn Taber, Bill How and Nancy Shippen. And loved others, who read, commented, advised, criticized, and supported: Jan Hoffman, Cathy Whitmire, Linda Chidsey, Marty Grundy, Elizabeth (Minga) Claggett-Borne. Lloyd Lee Wilson, Marian Baker, and Eric Edwards, sister and brothers in the ministry. Deborah Fisch read and commented wisely and supportively.

Further thanks are due for kind permission to use certain material: Chapter 22 first appeared in substance in *Friends Journal* 36 (Sept. 1990), pp. 5–9, and is used with permission. Quotations from W. Taber (1996), "Quaker ministry: the inward motion and the razor's edge," used with permission from F. Taber. Quotations from Skidmore (2003), *Strength in Weakness*, appear by permission; spelling and grammar as normalized in that book.

Finally, warm thanks to Fran Taber and Bill Taber for their comments and encouragement. Bill's friendship and ministry changed my life.

Some specific thanks are owed: I am very grateful for the discernment, care, thought and thoroughness that Marty Grundy brought to the task of editing this manuscript. Thanks also to Fran Taber for her foreword, and to Darcy Drayton for the painting that has been used on the cover, and which now takes its place in our private gallery. Finally, Barbara Hirshkowitz at the press made the process of book-producing a pleasure.

All these Friends have been of tremendous help, and words of thanks don't convey the vivid and special colors that surround each of them in my mind's eye. Blame none of them for any inadequacies you find in this book.

Scripture citations: All Bible quotations are from the King James version, unless otherwise noted.

And first, as to you, my beloved and much honoured brethren in Christ, that are in the exercise of the ministry: Oh! feel life in your ministry—let life be your commission, your well-spring and treasury on all such occasions; else you well know, there can be no begetting to God, since nothing can quicken or make people alive to God, but the life of God; and it must be a ministry in and from life, that enlivens any people to God. . . . and Oh! that there were more of such faithful laborers in the vineyard of the Lord! Never more need since the day of God.

WILLIAM PENN 1980, 67–8

Oh!, my dear sister, what awful ground a true gospel minister stands on in the sacred office! It puts me in mind of what the Majesty of Heaven said to Moses, "Put off thy shoes from off thy feet, for the place whereon thou standest is holy ground." Indeed, we must be thus unshod, as it were, to receive and communicate messages of grace. And for my part, I find, from time to time, the preparation as needful as if it had never been known before.

SARAH (LYNES) GRUBB 1863, 35

Introduction

Dear Friend,

We have no time but this present time to bear witness to the power of the Light to re-create the human heart, and thus transform our doing, our seeing, and our speaking. There is much tenderness and good will among us, but have we been baptized with fire, as well as the Holy Spirit? The quiet Quaker ways were discovered and inhabited so that we might live freely and passionately, faithful to the Spirit that moves according to its own imperatives. The path to that freedom and that radical availability is one of practice, but also of learning, and we need all the help we can get from our community, as well as from the essential leader, the Light of Christ experienced within.

In this learning and helping, we cannot neglect the power of words and ideas, though the aim is not powerful words, but lives filled more and more with God's power. The gospel ministry is ministry that speaks under obedience, from living inward experience of Christ's Spirit in its struggles to be brought forth in each of us, for the refreshment of its life in those that hear. This ministry has always been an essential nutrient for a vital spiritual testimony—to encourage and support the gathered community, to gather people to the community, and to turn others to the witness of Christ in their hearts, whether they join Friends or not.

Yet we have much to learn about how we can open so that our ministry can grow in diversity and power in our own times, and I believe that, in part, this means learning again about the gospel ministry as a service to which some of us are explicitly, obediently committed for a long period of time. There are many good treatments of "vocal ministry in the meeting for worship," but very few of them address what Friends have historically recognized as a calling to this service.

The important missing ingredient is the element of time, that is, what happens (and should happen) if a Friend should continue in this service, with specific intent, for a period of years.

As I have lived with this calling, and observed others doing so, I have become convinced that an exploration of this experience is also a way to understand some fundamental aspects of Quaker practice and theology. The gospel ministry, while unique in some ways, should be seen as complementary to all the other kinds of religious service that emerge in a community. I find it useful to speak of it as a "concern" in Friends' sense of that term. For this reason, an exploration of what it means to carry this concern for a length of time may well throw some light upon spiritual issues that may arise when one carries any spiritual concern for a period of years.

This topic has been addressed a few times in the past. Some years ago, Pendle Hill and the Tract Association of Friends published a reprint of the most famous treatment, Samuel Bownas' *Description of the Qualifications Necessary to a Gospel Minister.* I have received important help from this little book. Yet I have found a persistent leading to write something from the point of view of a modern Friend which might complement writings by Bownas and others on the topic.[1] I believe that something additional is needed, for several reasons.

Friends have much to offer the world, in their understanding of Christianity as well as in their social witness. A vibrant, diverse, and dedicated ministry has always been an important contributor to Friends' witness to the world, and to the health of Quaker spiritual life. Yet there is at present little understanding of ministry as a calling, as a long-term concern, among unprogrammed Friends. There is, moreover, great diversity of opinion about the nature and purpose(s) of vocal ministry, and its relationship to the Quaker spirituality rooted in expectant waiting worship.

In helping modern Friends and others revive a living ministry, books from earlier times can be valuable, but also have

---

[1] An extensive, though not complete, bibliography of relevant writings can be found at the end of this book.

limitations because of the difference between the times in which they wrote, and the times in which we live and read their words. Samuel Bownas' manual makes many assumptions about his audience which can hardly be made in these days. For example, he writes to people who are familiar with the idea of a calling to ministry; who are familiar with the work of ministers in intervisitation, family visits, opportunities and the like; who are familiar with the Bible, and who are used to seeing their own spiritual lives as a continuation of the biblical story; who assume that Friends are to be markedly different from those around them; who are familiar with the Quaker rhythms of worship and business daily, weekly, monthly, and throughout the year. In these and other ways, the Quaker culture out of which Bownas wrote is not the culture most of us inhabit.

Our world is very different from that in which Bownas lived and worshipped. The intervening 250 years have increased the prestige and accomplishments of science and technology, have seen the rise of capitalism and socialism, have seen an astonishing accumulation of wealth in the North, and have seen much of that wealth diverted to murderous weaponry on the one hand, and vacuous consumption on the other.

Even in the United States, the most church-going nation in the developed world, a primarily secular viewpoint, or its variant, American "national religion," is increasingly the common mindset, entrenched in the churches as well as other parts of society. This presents important, indeed fundamental challenges to those seeking to articulate a Quaker vision amidst the ideological complexity of the spiritual landscape. Furthermore, one consequence of the consumerism that is a key element of modern ideology is that one's choice of this or that spiritual path seems one more among many choices based on taste and utility. An essential element of this psychology is complete freedom of choice, we easily learn to desire to customize our religion in the same way we might customize our home sound systems, mixing and matching components as we like.

Most Friends in unprogrammed meetings are "convinced," and come to Friends both seeking what Friends have to offer, and bringing some provisional answers of their own from previous seeking. For this reason, we are very vulnerable to the "shopping" approach to spirituality. In this climate the integrity of Quaker spirituality, and the depth of the practical resources that it offers over time, are overlooked or unguessed, as Friends and those who come among us shop in the spiritual supermarket.

Under these conditions, the spiritual work required of a Friend who feels particular concern for the ministry is in some ways very different from that confronting her predecessors from previous centuries—though many of the old challenges remain as well. In the next chapter, I will try to be more specific about some of the challenges that appear to me to face a Friends minister who seeks to understand and follow the concern for gospel ministry in our present world and the Religious Society of Friends.

While I think that some of what follows may be valuable to anyone seeking to understand the Quaker way, I am particularly concerned for Friends in unprogrammed meetings who are willing to consider the possibility that the gospel ministry is for them a central, long-term "concern," or might become one. Of course, anyone in a meeting for worship is likely at some time or other to be pulled to their feet with a message for the meeting, and this openness is a precious aspect of our practice. As the disciplines say, "Do not assume that vocal ministry is never to be your part." In fact, I believe (and hope) that the considerations written here may be of value and interest to *any* Friend.

However, it has been part of our experience from the beginnings of our movement that for some people, the vocal ministry becomes a *concern*, which is carried for some length of time, possibly for life, and that the presence of such Friends concerned for the gospel ministry is a vital element nourishing the faithfulness of the whole body.

> we do believe and affirm that some are more particularly called
> to the work of the ministry and therefore are fitted of the Lord
> for that purpose, whose work is more constantly and particularly

to instruct, admonish, oversee, and watch over their brethren. (Barclay 2002 [1678], 274)

It is for these Friends that I am writing.

I use the term "gospel ministry" not primarily for continuity with the usage of earlier times, but rather to emphasize some important characteristics of the ministry as Friends have understood it. The gospel is the "power of God to salvation," it is the life and light of Christ at work, in characteristic ways,[2] to bring us into freedom from spiritual bondage. Gospel ministry is service whose goal is to encourage, support, push, or invite people to seek and respond to the guidance, teaching, and activity of that Light and Life at work in all, right now. It is not merely speaking words in meetings for worship, but, under a sense of obedience to the motions of the Spirit, using words, deeds, or silent striving to help others (and ourselves) forward to the more abundant life that Jesus sought for his disciples, his friends. This ministry can take many forms, as will be explored hereafter, but the goal is always the same.

> The main design of gospel ministry is to turn the children of men to the grace of God in themselves, which will teach them to work out their own salvation, and diligently to seek the Lord for themselves. (Griffith 1779, 128)

In what follows, you will find short essays on a range of topics. They are only loosely arranged in a sequence; this is intentional. My hope is that you will dip into this at need, and as if reading letters from a friend. I am not building to a specific point, but painting in the picture from all directions.

The reader will discover many stories and illustrations drawn from Quakerism of the past three and one half centuries (and will discover why I think this is important), but I must stress that this is not a nostalgic book. To the best of my ability, I am writing out of modern, lived experience, both of myself and of many other Friends that I know. However, our experience builds on the lives and testimony of many lives before us

---

[2] That is, the Spirit of Christ is not just any spirit, and where it is at work it produces specific effects that testify to their source.

which have shaped the Quaker path, and they still offer important lessons for current living. They are our contemporaries and companions in the Spirit, and the continuity of fellowship is both a source of strength and of challenge to us.

My language and my testimony is Christian. Friends do not and should not enforce doctrinal standards, but it is clear to me that Quakerism is an innovative, radical, and indeed, in John Punshon's phrase, "Alternative Christianity" (Punshon 1982). In these times we need to be forthright in articulating our understanding of life under the guidance of the Spirit of Christ—and what is characteristic of that Spirit as opposed to others. "See if your Christ be the same that was from everlasting to everlasting, or is he changed according to the times?"[3] While this should include listening and dialogue with Christians of other types, as well as people of all faiths, the indispensable minimum is an intentional, reflective, direct discipleship to that Spirit.

Our experience will raise questions and conflicts; Jesus never said, "Blessed are those who have figured everything out." Childlike we must accept both the blessings and clarity that come, and the experience of ignorance as well. As we make room for the Christ spirit, and it grows stronger and more fully within, we will be better able to say, and live, what we know, and wait upon the rest. This experience of obedience and of openness has always been at the core of the experience of gospel ministry, as well as Quaker practice in general; and the minister must be a persistent and patient student of that path and its mysteries of creation, healing, suffering, rejoicing, death, and rebirth.

Having said this much, I will mention that the reader will see God referred to variously in my own prose. I don't assign God a gender, but when I have Christ in mind, I sometimes use the masculine pronouns, though sometimes not. I have not edited the language of any quotations, except to shorten some (gaps are marked in the usual way . . .), and occasionally to supply missing words for clarity, marked by [square brackets].

[3] James Nayler, in Drayton 1994, 41.

I very much intend that this will be a living work, and will be glad for suggestions and fresh insights and examples which might contribute to an improved version in the future. (I certainly hope that as long as my concern continues, I will be learning, and hope to share that learning in case it may help.) For this reason, I encourage you, my brother or sister in this work, to write to me, and share your thoughts and ideas out of love and concern for all who share in the ministry of the Gospel.

Brian E Drayton

— BRIAN DRAYTON
MARCH 15, 2005
414 Pettingill Road
Lyndeborough, NH 03082
brian_drayton@terc.edu

Thou deep wader for the good of souls, this is wrote principally for thy sake, that thou mayest see others have gone the same way before thee, and be encouraged so as not to sink under thy burden. I found in the Lord's time (as thou wilt, if thou patiently holds on thy way) that tribulation worketh patience, and patience experience, and experience hope. (Griffith, 118)

1

The dilemma of gospel ministry in the twenty-first century

Anyone who feels a concern for the gospel ministry these days—that is, ministry that arises from, proclaims, and reaches to the life of the gospel as Friends have understood it—faces several challenges which can be discouraging, and call into question the very notion of such a concern. Some of these challenges are specific to modern Quaker culture, some are reflections of the broader society; many of them challenge the life of faith itself. Perhaps another way to say this is, we are often unsure of what the gospel is, and whether it should be preached, or its life encouraged; and we have a constricted view of what it may be. It behooves every Friend, but especially those who speak in ministry, to recognize and engage with these tensions honestly, with intellect, heart, and soul, because in them lie many of the spiritual challenges which we all face. The following are those which have seemed most pressing to me; doubtless you will think of others to add.

A tendency to restrict the room for divine activity in our lives

Friends as a group are as infected as most members of our society with a strong reliance on human reason and strength. Our institutions—schools, service organizations, and often even including our meetings for business—are constantly tempted to canvass the best ideas and opinions that are present, and then devise decisions in what might be called a business-like manner, with only a hazy view of how the decision grows out of and relates to the divine life among us. This is not because we do not care about it; but it tends to be only in moments of high stress, or in important decisions about big questions that we really take the time to seek deeply, feel after the life, and in a sense taste how our actions might tend towards more abundant life in the Holy Spirit. Yet we forget that our discernment is likely to be better when we come to such big issues, if we have been practicing on the small things, both in our meetings and in our daily life.

The fragmentation of the Quaker movement

The divisions among Friends are long-established historical trends, which have characteristic realizations in each nation. While in places like Britain or Kenya, the theological variations are held in uneasy solution within yearly meetings, in North America, these trends took on substantive expression in umbrella organizations such as Friends United Meeting, Evangelical Friends International, and Friends General Conference. These associations arose in response to a sincere desire for effective witness and mutual support, and as a partial gesture towards unity. They have also, to some extent, institutionalized faction. Each "branch" in North America has developed its preferred religious language, literature, customs, and organizations.

Of course in most meetings, and in every "branch," there are individual Friends who love to reach out to "the other," and cultivate a perspective that sees all varieties of Quakerism as fragments of a shattered whole. Yet in the absence of substantial intervisitation, with the increase in our individualism and the decrease in our understanding of true discipline under the Spirit, most of us most of the time are in a provincial state of mind.

For many Friends, and perhaps especially the majority of unprogrammed Friends, the consciousness of this remarkable diversity (and the tensions and dilemmas that arise from it) has made it hard to speak with any sense of confidence about the relationship between our subjective life, the central assertions and discoveries of Quakerism, and the life of the world at large. Respect for individual experience, which has been a fundamental Quaker value from the earliest times, is now accompanied by modern developments that loosen or eliminate our connections with our religious tradition, including the post-modern response to a diverse world. We find it hard or impossible to speak with joy and confidence out of a shared experience of the work of Christ in and through us. Early Friends were remarkably diverse as well, yet they still felt unity, not in their beliefs primarily, but in their understanding of their center, in the Light of Christ which was the key to their experience. George Fox, debating at Swarthmoor with a group of hostile clerics, drew a sharp distinction between his understanding of God's Truth as discovered and enacted, and the retreat to bare personal experience:

> I asked them whether any of them could say they ever had a word from the Lord to go and speak to such or such a people and none of them durst say so. But one of them burst out into a passion and said that he could speak his experiences as well as I; but I told him experience was one thing but to go with a message and a word from the Lord as the prophets and the apostles had and did, and as I had done to them, this was another thing. (Fox, in Nickalls 1952, 123)

A secular view of time

People have always been liable to become so absorbed in their business, family, and other affairs that they do not reserve substantive time for prayer and reflection. This is not a malady of the twenty-first century alone, but a persistent feature of human life. The sources of this busyness are many, and one may surmise that beyond a certain point it is not because of necessity. Rather, in activity we feel our reality. In some kinds of activity, we establish or reinforce our importance to others, or make an argument to ourselves about our own value. My activity is also a way of asserting that I am engaged with life, and therefore not (yet) threatened by death. Moreover, it cannot be denied that activity sometimes provides us with escape from ourselves, and also from confronting the Truth that is likely to be met in silence and stillness.

While these things are not new, it may well be that our modern society has created more means of distraction and empty activity than have ever existed before. By "empty" activity, I mean activity that in the end is a surrogate for learning, for relating, for prayer, for rest, or for some creative or necessary work. Our frequent lamentations about our busyness speak vividly of the effects on spiritual life of the many methods of communication that are now available to us, and in some eyes have become indispensable to the full life. How great a fear there is, in our culture, that we might not exercise every possible choice, or that we should ever accept any constraint upon our freedom! It is seen as a positive good always to be in reach of friends, family, work, the marketplace; and for most people, the only countervailing concern is not to overdo it. Moreover, in the activity of communication and participation in the culture, we find a defense against our fear of aloneness.

There is nothing that will kill a concern, and the growth of one's ability to carry it faithfully, more quickly than an overactive mind. Further, the habits of too much activity, too much stimulation, and too much communication, can keep us stunted spiritually, because words, events, and music can preempt the faculties of reason and reflection. That is why they can so effectively shield us from things we would rather not engage.

The consumer approach to religion

Since the beginning of the Quaker movement, people coming in to the Religious Society of Friends have brought with them all kinds of baggage—personal, social, theological; as a convinced Friend, I can attest to this personally. Commonly enough, we in-comers have unpacked these bags in a way that influenced the Quakerism we joined, or at least the Quakerism we were able to experience. Amelia Mott Gummere's study (1901) of the changes in Quaker dress over the centuries still stands as a valuable demonstration of the steady interchange between "the Society" and "the World."

However, the last 100 years have seen a remarkable, double change. On the one hand, the proportion of "convinced Friends" has become much larger than the proportion of

Friends who have grown up in the tradition (in some yearly meetings it is by far the largest group). On the other hand, Quakers of whatever genesis have become much more complete participants in the surrounding culture, which has become eclectic and consumer-oriented to an extreme, even with respect to spirituality and religion.

The consequent intensified sense of personal search in a global marketplace has made it possible for Friends to hunt diligently in many different traditions for knowledge and practices that give them some sense of comfort, insight, or renewal. I do not see that this is harmful in and of itself, and certainly I have been glad to learn from several traditions, including those I was raised in before I found Friends.

Yet there are costs as well as benefits deriving from this eclecticism, and especially for the ministry in unprogrammed worship. One of the most regrettable deficits has been the loss of a deep exploration of Quakerism's resources as a major spiritual path, which has its own costs for a person seeking to live out its commitments, and makes demands upon the adherent, pulling him or her out of a place of ease, rather than being a construction conformable in most things to his or her personal preferences. In previous times, Quakers spoke of the Cross, of the death of self, when explaining how the Spirit led them beyond their own preferences and habits. Modern Friends feel less comfortable with such language, but the reality of the experience is a foundation of any claim that we are experiencing some aspect of divine Truth, and engaged with a living God that is not created in our own image. It takes time to understand the implications of the Quaker understanding of the life of the soul, and much experimental testing against the challenges of life. Coming into "that life and power that takes away the occasion of all wars"—reaching to that life, and making it yours, is the work of a lifetime. It is that Life, as sought, struggled with, learned from, and embodied, which is where words come from which nourish, guide, warn, encourage the soul.

Uncertainties about leadership, and communities inexperienced in caring for gifts and callings

We are uncomfortable about the idea of leadership—more concretely, we are uneasy about having leaders or being leaders—and we are not clear how leadership should look among Friends. This discomfort is widely recognized, as is the need for the identification and support of authentic leadership; there is therefore a small but solid literature addressing the need for the right nurture of leaders among us. There are many reasons for our reluctance. One source of the problem which is relevant to the exercise of a concern for the gospel ministry rests upon a misconception about what leadership is. Too often, it is related in our minds to the exercise of power or influence, as in political or corporate life. This is not at all the kind of leadership that Friends' ministry should be providing, and where it does look like that, either the Friend in question is exercising dual roles, or there is a failure of the Friend and the community to shape a right calling.

There is no question that some Friends who have grown to positions of authority have exercised it injuriously at times. It is common enough to retell stories of times in the past when recorded ministers threw their weight around, even to the point of covering up crimes committed by other leaders. James Jenkins, an English Friend of the eighteenth century, describes how some ministering Friends (as well as many of the elders) assumed a kind of authoritarian tone that he (understandably) found repellent:

> I have noticed, that at the Yearly Meeting, we had the company of Samuel Emlen, Nicholas Waln, George Dillwyn, and John Pemberton [all visitors from the United States] . . . who, altho' they often preached excellently to us, yet, in the meetings for discipline, they frequently took the lead . . . in that sort of dicta-torial meddlement in the business of the meetings, which is sel-dom taken by *modest* strangers—even to apposite remarks, answers frequently abrupt, and sometimes rude, were given by them, and if this happened to provoke a rejoinder of censure or reproof, they stood up, and defended each other, with all the

faithfulness, and zeal of true, confederacy. (Jenkins 1984, 185; spelling and punctuation as in the original, but the abbreviations of first names expanded)

More often, a less dark arrogance still caused harm to individuals and meetings, and damaged the credibility of the ministry. For example, James Jenkins described how the prominent minister Catherine Phillips,

> like a great Autocratrix, sometimes governed, and sometimes without succeeding attempted to govern. . . . To an austerity of conduct that had much the appearance of domination, she added a sourness of temper, that disgraced the woman, and assumed an over-bearing consequence which (at least I thought) an humble minister of the Gospel could not assume. (Jenkins 1984, 118)

Of course, abuses that can be recounted under the old system of "select meetings" of ministers and elders in past eras are not unknown today, in modern form, and in more modern arrangements among Friends. People are very liable to prefer to have their own way when they can get it, and as hierarchical creatures, humans (including Friends) slip very easily into habits of command or control, overt or covert.

Yet such abuses are not typically the biggest problem facing a meeting, in regard to the identification and support of gifts. More often, we are over-cautious, and unsure how to proceed. Meetings may not see a need for any care of their members' gifts; or they may fear that by addressing them somehow, they will encourage the growth of undesirable distinctions, hierarchies, preferences, or egotism. Furthermore, we can see how purposefully undertaking some care of the gifts among our members could lead to mistaken judgments, even conflict.

It is a severe misfortune that for such reasons we are backward about accepting and nurturing gifts that can serve the life of the Spirit among us. As a result, many gifts are not cultivated and disciplined as they might be, and the life of the meeting is thereby diminished.

> Does it matter that we have largely lost the corporate dimension of ministry? I think the answer is a resounding "Yes!" because the lack

of corporate involvement and mutual accountability devalues the gift and diminishes the minister's effectiveness. It discounts the seriousness and awe of recognizing a gift being given by God to the group. We are all spiritually impoverished. (Grundy 1999, 14)

I believe that this unease and unskill at nurturing gifts is particularly acute with respect to Friends who carry a concern for a long period of time, and even more so for Friends with a concern for gospel ministry. As a result, at present we have few living examples as patterns (or, I suppose, warning signs) from which an individual seeking to follow the concern, or a meeting seeking to nurture it, can draw guidance.

A skepticism about ministry as a calling

There are some who have felt that since any of us can at times be called to offer the ministry needed in a meeting for worship, there is no need to ascribe to the idea that there can be a separate "calling" to the ministry as a concern. While at first this makes sense, and accords with our increasingly democratic conception of the Society and the commonwealth of God, it does not comport well with scripture or with the experience of Friends over the past several centuries. However, the initial plausibility of this assertion is a warning and a reproof to us all, because it suggests that fewer and fewer Friends have seen evidence in their own or others' lives of the fruits of faithfulness to this concern. They don't see evidence, or perhaps don't know what to look for.

As William P. Taber writes:

In our time . . . many more people take occasional responsibility for the ministry, but there are relatively few ministers who have gone through the long and arduous experience of learning by discerning that was typical of most ministers (sometimes called public Friends) of the eighteenth century. (Bownas 1989, Taber introduction, xxiv)

Lucia Beamish writes:

"Of how many could it be said today, as it was said of Benjamin Seebohm . . . that 'his ministry was the most characteristic thing about his life; more than anything else it was evidently that for which he lived.'" (Taber introduction, Beamish 1963, 344)

Perhaps one factor at play here is that a misunderstanding of the nature of the work of the ministry has led to its impoverishment, attenuation, neglect, or abuse, and hence to a real aversion to attempts to renew, revive, or otherwise acknowledge its value in our community. It is for this reason that I find it more effective and useful instead to speak of those for whom the gospel ministry is a concern that they carry. Modern Friends have many ways of talking about and working with concerns, and making appropriate use of these ideas and practices can help us explore the gospel ministry in our day concretely and practically. It also enables us to consider what this concern has in common with other concerns—and in what ways it is unique.

The corrosion of false religion

We are in a time when faith is hard to sustain, and when many cultural voices, both secular and religious, describe kinds of faith, and versions of Christianity, which feel deeply unsatisfactory when put to the tests of mind, heart, or soul. Religion is portrayed as a system of doctrines, or as a system of social control, or as the ally of the state, or the market, or of this or that party. Or again it is said to be a matter of purely private and subjective concern, an arrangement of your mental furniture according to your own taste, but irrelevant to any one else.

Furthermore, many people think that they have tried Christianity, and that it doesn't work. There are many ways in which humanity is ailing, and one of these ways is a kind of heartsickness, which one notices in thinking about Christianity and its witness in the world, because the *Christianoi*, the little Christs, have so often sided against the Gospel, while denying their failures all the while.

Who will trust their testimony, who will trust *my* testimony, if it is given in Christ's name anymore? Remember John Woolman's dream, in which he says

I was then carried in spirit to the mines, where poor oppressed people were digging rich treasures for those called Christians, and heard them blaspheme the name of Christ, at which I was grieved, for his name to me was precious. Then I was informed that these heathens were told that those who oppressed them were the followers of Christ, and they said amongst themselves: If Christ directed them to use us in this sort, then Christ is a cruel tyrant. (Woolman 1971, 185–6)[4]

Yet Friends can, if we dare, uphold a different view, even while acknowledging the strong reasons many have for rejecting religion, or Christianity. Our religion is based on our friendship with Christ, walking as children of the Light, and should lead us into a recognizable life. True religion should bear the fruits of the spirit: love that casts out fear, joy, peace, long-suffering, gentleness, goodness, faith, meekness, temperance, justice, simplicity, and the commitment to overcome evil with good, and not to return evil for evil. None other can we accept. We are empowered to bear these fruits as we welcome the birth of Christ's Spirit in us, and allow that life to put to death "whatever is of a nature contrary to itself," as we wait in silence, worship and work in fellowship, and act on the guidance we are given. We are called to holiness, and of a kind that (for all the diversities of our natures and gifts) is given characteristic shape by the nature and work of Christ's spirit.

---

[4] The preceding three paragraphs taken from Drayton 1996.

2

The challenge of holiness

It is urgent that we all be about the business of becoming holy; we have not a moment to lose. We are invited to lead a life in collaboration with the spirit of Christ working in us, in order to escape the bondage of sin, each according to our gifts and talents, each in our own situation—what are we waiting for? We need to see the challenge in its full extent, and take it up as fully as we can. This is no drudgery, even if it is hard work, because the reward is freedom from fear, and a realization of our connection to an inexhaustible store of light and life.

Furthermore, while it is not something that we can do in our own power, we do not need to: we open to it, when we feel that we need and want to respond to God's continuing invitation. "As the hart panteth for the water brooks, so panteth my soul after thee, O God" (Ps. 42). This is enough to start with; we may have always had the longing in just these simple terms, or we may come to it through an inner weariness, or a revulsion or impatience about our life as it currently is. Once we look toward the Light with desire and a little trust, we find that it shows us an opening way. Then we enter into the experimental life in the Spirit. We come to know our darkness, in a way that is no longer superficial and glib—it becomes harder just to say, "Well, nobody's perfect, of course," because we realize it is a false answer to a wrong question, and the realization stabs sharply. We come also to feel how the Spirit can work re-creation within us, that the ocean of light and life can flow over the ocean of darkness.

At first, it may be that all we can manage is to stand quietly in the vicinity of the teacher—we may have no more strength than that, or perhaps we cannot see what to do. In his presence, however, as well as through his teaching, we start to get the hang of things, the way to look at our lives, and at the world we inhabit, and we start to see what we need to do, or stop doing, in order to feel more in harmony with his life, to free the Seed of it, and encourage the growth of it in our feeling and thinking, willing and doing.

It does not come all at once. The realization of what we need, and the deciding whom to follow, may be an event that we can identify with date and time. It may steal over us, however, as God's silent working in us has found some quiet welcome, before we are fully aware.

When the merchant had sold everything and bought the land in which his pearl of great price was hidden, then what? He still had to manage his business, be a husband and father, interact with his friends and neighbors, make his choices and his prayers. We are always beginning, and so we are always vulnerable to discouragement, and tempted to get control of things and rush ahead to the finish line. The more aware we are, the more likely it is that we will see and feel obstacles and struggles. At our first taste of God's life and power, our early feeling of progress, we naturally can't see how much we are really beginners, newcomers to a way of life being forged in the midst of established patterns, needs, and assumptions— both in our selves, and in all those we live among. So naturally it will happen that as we make more room for the new, we encounter unrenovated places in us and our relationships and activities. Our new sensitivity makes us painfully aware of incongruities, but how to resolve them? Sometimes it is a matter of simple "surgery"—I will not, and need not, do that any more ("if thy right hand offend thee, cut it off." Mt. 5:30); I will not say or speak such things, I can no longer think in that way ("If thy right eye offend thee, pluck it out." Mt. 5:29).

Sometimes, however, it's not so direct, and there is tension, fear, anger, pain, or simple confusion. Remember, though, that the Spirit "takes its kingdom with entreaty, and not with contention, and keeps it by lowliness of mind," and be willing to wait, not knowing, until way opens. God, who is drawing you, will remain a steady guide, and often a compassionate one.

I remember when I first met with my Guide. He led me into a very large and cross [path], where I was to speak the truth from my heart—and before I used to swear and lie, too, for gain. "Nay, then," said I to my Guide, "I mun leave thee here; if thou leads me up that lane, I can never follow. . . . Here I left my Guide and was filled with sorrow, and went back to the Weeping Cross; and I said, if I could find my good Guide again, I'll follow Him, lead me whither He will. So here I found my Guide again, and began to follow Him and . . . got to the end of this lane, though with difficulty. But now my Guide began to lead me up another lane, harder than the first, which was to bear my testimony in using the plain language. This was very hard; yet I said to my Guide, "Take my feeble pace, and I'll follow Thee as fast as I can. Don't outstretch me, I pray Thee. So by degrees I got up here.(Luke Cock, "Sermon of the Weeping Cross, London Yearly Meeting, Faith and Practice, #42)

We are always beginning, and so we are always vulnerable to discouragement, and tempted to get control of things and rush ahead to the finish line, rather than to keep in step with our Guide.

Yet as you keep on, day by day, watching, acting, reflecting, learning from success and from error, you will find that you have actually been carried further along the path than you thought. When you stop and ask, What reason have I to give thanks? you will discover that you are notably more free, more available, less wrathful, more open and inwardly aware, readier to follow a good impulse, than you were before. "Fear not, little flock, it is your Father's good pleasure to give you the kingdom of heaven." (Lk 12:32) And so it is very important to take seriously the admonition to "give thanks continually," because the grateful heart is teachable and not self-sufficient.

Now, Friends have always felt that some progress in this life is essential to the growth of the gift in gospel ministry. It is not that a minister is better than anyone else, or has an unusual allotment of holiness. On the other hand, one whose calling is to be ready to speak or act from the most essential root of things, "to the refreshment of the children of Light," must ground the concern for this service in a more fundamental calling, the calling that comes to all of us to be holy.

Therefore, if you profess or suspect that you are called to the ministry, you have to take seriously the call to a devout life, and become experienced in all the complexities that this deeper calling entails. Without a committed immersion in the life, we cannot feel after the life in others, where it may be encouraged, or where it may be chained down. We need to become knowledgeable about the difference between the voice of God and of Self and culture. Otherwise, we will be even more prone to preach ourselves, rather than the Gospel—the power of God to liberation—than people usually are. The minister must more and more seek to be an experienced soul: and thus, I agree with Bownas, that in addition to the calling of the Spirit, some authentic experience of the Spirit's work in us is the fundamental qualification. As William Taber wrote:

> When the call is truly recognized, the budding minister— which could be any or all of us—comes to know, deep in the gut, that we are called to live in that amazing reality which was before all words were, and that that reality wants to transform us into a profound wholeness. . . . The budding minister—and remember, that can include all of us—may have one, or even several profound experiences of transformation, graced empowerment and a deep sense of dedication, but no one of these moments of sanctification (if I may use the term) is final and absolute—there is always more to learn, and we continue to learn and grow as long as we live.
>
> This yearning for conversion of life and manners, this daily and persistent turning and returning to the Light, this unashamed openness for sanctification, and for what earlier Friends called the inward work of Christ is, in my experience, the only foundation of an effective and life-changing ministry. (Taber 1996)

Now, I freely confess that it is hard to look at your friends and intimates, who know you well, and say "I am seeking to be holy." Yet is this not the one thing needful, to recognize our need and longing to dwell immersed in the divine life? If you get down to the little, sweet springs of life, you will find your proper objections, and your prideful objections, and your temptations to inflation or false abasement, and your embarrassment, will melt, and you will be anchored enough to say in a voice that has truth in it, "I have found Him, the Seed and Source and companion—O taste and see that the Lord is good!"

3
What does the ministry do?

Thou shalt love the Lord thy God with all thy heart, and with all thy soul, and with all thy mind. This is the first and greatest commandment, and the second is like unto it: Thou shalt love thy neighbor as thyself. (Mt. 22:37)

How shall we live this love, to God and our fellow humans? When you ask yourself honestly how free you are in your love to God and your neighbor, do you not have to report a partial and intermittent success? It is typical of human experience that our sense of the divine life, and our ability to speak and act from it, will flow strongly sometimes, but then at other times weaken and grow remote, so that the version of ourselves that felt fervent and expansive with the motion of the Spirit seems strange to us, and when we are feeling our own strength of mind, will, and body, the strength of the Spirit, so very different in its flavor, seems almost a delusion.

John Burnyeat wrote in his journal of this spiritual high and low tide:

> I found, that as my Heart was kept near the Power, it kept me tender, soft, and living; And besides, I found as I was diligent in eying of it, there was a constant sweet Stream, that run [sic] softly in my soul, of Divine Peace, Pleasure, and Joy. . . . And furthermore, I did observe, that if I neglected, or let my Mind out after anything else more than I ought, and so forgot this, I began to be like a Stranger, and saw that I soon might lose my interest in these Riches and Treasure, and true Common-wealth of God's Spiritual Israel. (Burnyeat 1691, 20)

Our spiritual condition relates intimately to that of our spiritual community. When we are dwelling solidly in the divine life, we lend strength to our friends who may be encountering the challenges of life. Very importantly, we are also storing up reserves of nourishment for the darker, harder times, when joy and freedom seem far away. At those times, in fact, the faithfulness of our friends, in word, deed, or example, may be the only key into those memories and learned truths which can reassure and revive us during our times of feeling lost or cold.

A concern for the ministry is a calling to be intentionally available to put our experience of the divine light and life at the disposal of others, for their refreshment and encouragement. If we accept the calling, then it is a commitment to redouble our inward watchfulness, so that we grow in faithfulness, and grow in our ability to serve. As we gain more of this inward experience, we find an increase in the clarity with which we are able to desire, pray for, serve, and rejoice at, the growth of the love to God and neighbor as it appears in anyone. This in turn feeds the life of the group, and invites others to come and see. "It is a living ministry that begets a living people; and by a living ministry at first we were reached and turned to the Truth. It is a living ministry that will still be acceptable to the church and serviceable to its members."[5]

A faithful ministry will support the growth of this love but different people may have particular gifts which reach to one or another person's condition at any particular time; and anyone may contribute, as the Holy Spirit moves them, and makes use of their experience and gifts, at a particular time and place. So we need many voices in the ministry, and Friends need to dwell deeply enough, and with enough interest in the welfare of souls, that when words are called forth, they are the fruit not only of deep feeling, or deep thought, but deep experience of life and life in the Spirit. Isaac Penington wrote:

> The end of the ministry is not only to gather, but also to preserve and build up what is gathered, even to perfection. And the soul being (especially at first, if not for a long time) weak and babish, not so fully acquainted with the measure of life (having had but some touches and demonstrations of it, but not being gathered fully into it, nor rooted and settled in it); I say, the soul

---

[5] Testimony concerning John Banks by Somerset Quarterly Meeting 1711, quoted by A.N. Brayshaw in *The Quakers*, 1969 [1953], 247.

in this state, hath as much need of the ministry to preserve, direct, and watch over it in the truth, as to gather it out of the world. (Penington 1995–7, "Some queries concerning the order and government of Christ," 2:368)

It may not seem clear why the ministry is so useful an instrument of spiritual formation in our meetings, if you have not considered how complex a process the growth of spiritual maturity is—how various the paths each of us may take, and yet how many similar patterns and trials there are. Penington points out that outward helps are important, as we pass through the stages of spiritual growth. Furthermore, we are all liable to be reduced to "weak and babish" states, needing to be again gathered into the measure of life, so that the help of Friends is needful for us all at times. Barclay makes the plain point that people get help from people, even if the primary source of help is the light of Christ:

> For though God do [*sic*] principally and chiefly lead us by His Spirit, yet He sometimes conveys His comfort and consolation to us through His children whom He raises up and inspires to speak or write a word in season whereby the saints are made instruments in the hand of the Lord to strengthen and encourage one another. (Barclay 2002 [1678], 75; Prop. III)

It is sometimes hard to grasp this because events in our spiritual lives may be very brief indeed, and yet they may count for much in shaping our attitudes, hopes, or understandings about the soul-life. Therefore, it is worth reminding yourself to give attention to inward events for their content, and seek for their meaning, not looking at them with the everyday measures of minutes or days, nor measuring them by outward rules of success. Though indeed we will know the truth of our own or others' spiritual lives by their fruits, yet the fruit that may come from a particular fleeting event, perhaps even a secret one, may not be evident to the observer (nor even to the participant) for a long time.

Therefore, when we enter prayer or undertake a service for others' benefit, we need to be aware of the precious complexity and individuality of each soul, and be wary of overconfidence that we understand enough, and know the right answer. Often we do not. Too often our praying, saying, and doing do not reflect this attitude of respect, and the acknowledgement that (despite our best faithfulness) it is God's work going on in the other, not ours, and our longing is for that work to go forward.

It is good to consider the effects of ministry more specifically. For you to whom I'm writing, it is good also to consider, prayerfully, each of the effects described below.

First, each of them represents a basic need of human souls, and part of the work of the ministry is seeking under the Lord's guidance to feel after others' conditions.

Second, if these notes are not sounded in your meeting, or the meetings you frequent, it is good to pray that if need arises, someone will be drawn to see and respond to it. Your praying may help you become aware of gifts that you can encourage.

Third, this thinking and praying may also enlarge your own availability and concern, and you may find that your own service changes in response.

Perhaps it goes without saying, that while "the ministry" has the various effects discussed here, it may not be the case that they all are found in the ministry of any one individual!

Convicting, diagnosis

The ministry can help bring people to a sense of need, of the distance between their current condition and a life of adequacy in the light of Christ. Quaker preaching often mounted a powerful challenge to recognize and abandon self-sufficiency and dependence upon human strength in the face of our bondage to sin and the hardness and inaccessibility of our hearts to the love and justice of God. Indeed, an engagement in this conflict was the first theater of the Lamb's War. How often it is reported that a meeting was dipped into a state of brokenness and tenderness, often in the silent exercise of the gathered meeting, but sometimes facilitated by the faithful words of ministry. In these times, when a God-derived message is delivered faithfully, people can be awakened into concern, and convinced that they have found a path to a God-saturated life, a life freed from bondage. Thus individuals and groups can be aroused and gathered.

This is important even in meetings where most are members of the Religious Society. Many, having once found their way among us, and taken root in a meeting, then in a way cease moving forward, as though they had really reached a destination, when in fact their journey has just begun. Even among weighty Friends, a sleepiness can overtake the spirit. The words of one who has been overcome with a fresh sense of the lively and transformative operation of the Spirit can recall the comfortable, or sleepy, or untender, to a sense of presence, and a rejuvenation of their dedication and availability to the Spirit's guidance.

Encouraging, comforting

Of course, there are those who are doing their best to follow the light as they can see it, and are actively engaged in their spiritual lives, and yet are in need of refreshment and perhaps guidance along the way. While the teacher is Christ among us, it is a blessing that his counsel and encouragement sometimes come through the voice of a sympathizing fellow-traveller. It is an encouragement to know that Jesus was tempted in all things even as we are, but also to find that we are reached by the words of a living experience of temptation or trial, and perhaps of failure, such as we are feeling, and in that to hear also how the Lord's power was finally found. "God has given me the tongue of the taught." (Isaiah 50:4)

Connecting current personal experience with tradition and scripture, and articulating from the Quaker position

If God is at work among us, and we seek a fullness of the life of Christ in us, then our own daily experiences, trials, successes, and challenges are in some relation to this divine activity. If we affirm that God is not many but one, then our own individual spiritual experience should have some relation to the experience of others. We are not the only, nor the first, nor the last, to encounter (to our trouble and our joy) the inward motions of the divine life and, in fact, our understanding of our spiritual experience is enriched and given additional meaning by recognizing this, and seeking to understand its implications. We are part of a story, which includes both our own personal plot lines, and the larger, grander ones of the times in which we live—both the good and the evil, both the world of wonders and the world of suffering that surround us. All of this is also part of the story of God's calling to us, to live free from darkness, and free towards justice and love: the drama of salvation. This is a story in which millions have participated!

Penington, again:

> [Another] great help, which in the tender mercy of the Lord I have had experience of, is sobriety of judgment. Not to value or set up mine own judgment, or that which I account the judgment of life in me, above the judgment of others, or that which is indeed life in others. For the Lord hath appeared in others, as well as to me; yea, there are others who are in the growth of his truth, and in the purity and dominion of his life, far beyond me. Now for me to set up, or hold forth, a sense or judgment of a thing in opposition to them, this is out of the sobriety which is of the truth. Therefore, in such cases, I am to retire, and fear before the Lord, and wait upon him for a clear discerning and sense of his truth, in the unity and demonstration of his Spirit with others, who are of him, and see him. (Penington 1995–7, 2:371–2)

For this reason, it is a great help when ministry helps us see how to connect our own stories with those of scripture and Quakerism. This can be through building a bridge linking our language with the language of the Bible or early Friends. It may come in messages that "open" the scriptures in fresh ways, with the result that this great resource is more accessible and valuable to us than it was before. It may come in messages that shed fresh light upon Quaker testimonies and spiritual practice, enabling some to find new commitment, or enabling them to grapple more effectively with difficulties they have been feeling. We are to love the Lord with heart and soul and strength and mind. Ministry that comes from the life, and points to the life, in a way that helps our intellect or imaginations is often a great blessing.

Setting social and political events in spiritual context; pointing towards greater faithfulness in prophetic witness in the world.

So, too, is ministry that helps us make sense of the times in which we live, and how social and political trends are related to spiritual concerns. As Christians, we are called not to be conformed to the world, but to be transformed by the renewal of our minds, hearts, and wills (by the inward work of Christ). While part of our task as members of human society is to be enculturated, to understand the norms and ways of our people, our spiritual calling requires us to get free of those same conventional norms and commitments. In fact, it is only by knowing them well, and being freed from them, that we can see and understand the truth about the costs of institutions and society, and the ways in which they exert power over us, limiting our response to the Spirit, and accepting half-hearted attempts to live more deeply.

Some ministry can help us understand the nature of these tensions and the ways to overcome them in more faithful lives and witness, lives and witness that have power. Friends have from the beginning rejected the notion that this is an exclusively individual, inward experience, but rather have seen it as inseparable from a battle against social and political evil externally. As one Friend wrote, trying to explicate the connection between the "inner" and "outer" facets of the Lamb's War,

> The life engaged in the Lamb's War is tendered and opened to injustice and violence outwardly as well as inwardly. The human soul, your soul, can be seen as a nexus, a confluence, or focus of forces tending both to your good and ill. Some of the evils can be seen as external—sources of fear, oppression, or distraction. Others are apparently inward—anger, self-indulgence, and so on. Yet we are so constructed that we and our environment interpenetrate. Inward and outward forces activate or counteract each other. Because it is this kind of meeting place, the human

soul is an appropriate battlefield upon which to begin the war against "outward" evils in the world. More than this—if the battle remains unfought in any soul, then in our unredeemed regions, seeds of sin and death lie as in an incubator, from which they can spread abroad anew. The Lamb's War against the man of sin, in which we use the weapons of Jesus, acting at first upon our little, inward stage, is as well a social and indeed revolutionary act. (Drayton 1994, 4)

4
What does it mean to carry a concern?

The Quaker use of the word "concern" reflects our understanding about how God works through humans: it is a key element of Quaker spirituality, by which the Spirit engages with the world in creation, mercy, testimony, action. In the matrix of prayer, or in some other way, a matter comes before your mind which feels important, urgent, or pre-possessing. It may be you may become aware of a particular group of people whom you are drawn to, or you may become riveted by an issue requiring action or service. It is easy to name such subjects for a concern—John Woolman's concern for slaves, peace work, work for racial justice, or environmental protection.

A concern is more than subject matter, however, more than an area of interest or of passion, because it is accompanied (sooner or later) by a sense of duty: something is required, and at the Lord's hand. Part of your discernment must be, is it required of *me*, or does my heightened sensitivity enable me to see someone else who should be encouraged to consider it?

If it is required of me, then I should ask: Now, or in the future? Does a particular action come to mind, or must I spend time in preparation and inquiry before taking it up? How shall I get advice on this from my Friends? What are the risks, and the opportunities, that may come with this concern?

At some point, you come to the conclusion that this is something for which you must make adequate time in your life; the meaning of "adequate" will depend on the nature of the concern. Concerns come in all shapes and sizes, durations and levels of disturbance; they may be acute or chronic. That is, a concern may take the form of a long-term commitment (like a concern to be a faithful Friend, as you understand it, or to be active in race relations, or to take care of the meeting property), or it may be a short-term thing, a single action to be accomplished. Nevertheless, you become convinced that to maintain your sense of spiritual integrity, or to make way for some new inward growth, you must make room for, give attention to, this duty. "Making room" does not necessarily mean adding new things to your agenda. Rather, it is likely that some things will have to be set aside, and in some degree your whole organization of your time, self-care, work, and relationships may be affected, in order to ensure faithfulness.

For some people, the gospel ministry is such a concern. Any Friend may share in the meeting's vocal or silent ministry, of course. Many (it is to be hoped) will feel a deepening commitment to worship, study, reflection, and service in the meeting. The vocal ministry, however, can itself become a concern for some people, sustained for years or for life. If you are such a person, then the concern becomes an integral part of your spiritual path, for as long as the concern remains with you; it is a path of learning, of service, of consecration, of collaboration, of humility, of listening. As with all long-term concerns, you can learn better and better to be faithful to the concern, consonant with your gifts and openings. You will learn to know your authentic kind of service, your voice, and your limits.

It is important to be aware that intentionality about the ministry can open you to a whole range of temptations and challenges, perhaps especially because it is a public function. It "lets in self:" ego, self-approval (or self-criticism), considerations of status, and many other such things will need to be recognized, acknowledged, and overcome. If you don't do this work, your service will be harmed or prevented, and do harm to others as well as yourself, spiritually. I have come to see that the concern for the ministry is not a "calling to preach." At its heart, though this may take a long time to discover, it is a state of mind which is preoccupied with the fate of the Seed, Christ, in the hearts of men and women, coupled with a sense of responsibility to encourage and support others in their spiritual lives, and to use the powerful tools of language in this work of support, articulation, clarification, encouragement, and so on. Where is the life of Christ growing strongly, and producing good fruit? Where is it repressed or ignored or devalued? What may help someone become more aware of the motions of this life, and more responsive to it? What in our practice feeds or inhibits the growth in the spirit? Where do we fool ourselves, and how can we become more honest, direct, and teachable? How does this relate to our social settings, our economic or aesthetic lives, our relation to the earth, our politics? When and where can I serve to help others turn to and dwell in the light? What must I do to serve more effectively, conveying less of self and more of God? Even as I become more aware of the griefs of evil and folly, how can I dwell more in love, in gratitude, in fearlessness? How can I help people to see and rejoice in the evidences of Christ's life at work?

5

On discipleship and finding your way to the cross

The core and essence of a sustained calling in the ministry is this: to learn more and more to listen, pray, live, and act on behalf of the life of God where it is at work and where it is imprisoned in your fellow human beings.

You may not recognize this way of life in yourself yet. You may be reading this book because you find yourself often standing and speaking in meeting, or giving talks to groups of Friends, or otherwise exercising leadership, and wondering whether there is something yet to be learned about this activity. Is there a deeper place to speak from, a deeper kind of work to undergo? There are many ways in which one discovers this path, and many shapes it will take in different lives, suited to different personalities and situations.

Yet if the gift is to grow in usefulness, you will find yourself drawn into a path of learning in which new depths and dimensions are constantly revealed to you.

In following any purpose, we encounter obstacles and unexpected challenges. In seeking to render service to the life of God in the people, these obstacles are often of a very painful kind, because they are often our own limitations, weaknesses, and self-delusions—or the same kinds of discouraging elements in your friends, the ones for whom you feel concerned.

Sometimes you will feel that the whole enterprise of religion is a sham and a distraction, one that has caused more harm than good in human history. Sometimes you will feel that, while your own sense of commitment seems strong, others' is lukewarm, insufficient, half-hearted, shallow, and unresponsive to you or to others you value. Sometimes people directly oppose you and things you care deeply about, for reasons that seem discouragingly materialistic and self-serving.

Again, you might find yourself feeling that, even if your whole meeting, or the whole Religious Society of Friends, were as faithful as possible, all its efforts could not counter the vast oceans of darkness, folly, and grief that seem to threaten the sweetness of life in the modern world. You may find God distant, or not find God at all.

Such considerations, of course, may be rooted in some actuality, but whether your diagnosis is correct or not, you will find such perceptions a great danger and burden, because of the fruit they naturally bear in the human heart. Roadblocks and discouragements like these are often the occasion to discover in oneself a spirit of anger or of judgment, rejection and hopelessness. By comparison with the weight of these feelings, and the pungently distasteful aspects of oneself and one's whole species, the little, pure, sweet thing that is the life of God inwardly perceived seems weak and insubstantial at best.

Yet you may well find that you cannot leave behind the taste of this divine life that you have had, and cannot discount the joy and integrity that it has produced in others, and perhaps even in yourself sometimes. Then you cannot do anything else but return to hope, and long for that life to be a greater and greater feature of your own and others' experience; and so you return to your concern, to live and act in such a way as to make more and more room for that life.

Your travels in the wisdom of reason, and the wisdom found in the darkness of the heart, do not leave you unmarked, however, even in such a time of return—and how abrupt and short-lived sometimes are the changes in our inward weather! Against your hopes and commitments to the light, you have a fresh perception of what an inadequate person you are, how hypocritical you are, how little your energy is, or how inept are your attempts to serve, comfort, and support. You may also find, even in your turn towards hope, that your bleak diagnosis of the spiritual state of your friends and meetings is realistic, and confirmed by your discovery of the same shabby conditions in yourself.

In dilemmas like this, when I have felt doors shut to God in myself or others, and yet can hear the pleading voice of the visitor still asking for entry, I have come to see how the cross, as Friends understand it, is a matter for joy, and a creative path forward. This is not because of the doctrine that Jesus' substitutionary death on the cross outside Jerusalem wiped away the pain of sin for me and you, but rather because Christ is still about his Father's work of liberation right now, if we will cooperate with it. It is important here to consider the process of coming to the cross, because it is by this path that Friends have understood that we each participate in God's work of liberation. It is also in this way that we are enabled to help each other along the same path.

We tend to go through life feeling at ease with ourselves on most points, but to the extent we seek to visit the Lord's presence in stillness, this ease will sometimes be disturbed. When the light shows us some new place where the life of God is oppressed, blocked, or denied in us, whether by "human nature" or by ingrained habits, deep-rooted needs, or past wounds, we are given a choice once again: for that life, or against it. In our desire to choose life, however, it is all too easy to fall into schemes for the removal of the roadblock by will power, psychology, and good planning. This approach is not likely to succeed. You may be very strong-willed, but the strength of the will comes to an end, sooner or later; so, too, do cleverness, education, and planning eventually reach their limits.

When you see what the problem is, at that point bring it into the light. Stop seeking for more problems, and don't make plans or react yet, such as a different kind of work, of recognition, acknowledgement, and the removal of compulsions. Sit still until you can feel the presence, quiet and peaceful, and then introduce into that circle of light the difficult or ugly thing you wish to confront. In your persistent waiting for this moment of stillness and confidence, you will find and feel the work of the Cross, the little "death" or pruning through which we relinquish something which blocks the formation of Christ within.

It may take many minutes, or many days of minutes, before you can in quietness look this particular evil in the eye, acknowledge it, and move through self-judgment, anger, shame or whatever else is stirred up in you. The "crucifixion" or "death" of this attachment is located in this struggle to see honestly, and then to take the path to freedom from it. During this time of transition, of waiting and persistence towards that moment when the dark thing can stand clearly in the light, you will learn more about its nature. You will understand how deeply it may be rooted in yourself, and how it has had some function or history, which makes it an integral part of you, and just why it's so hard to get past. Here, in your prayer, there will be time for grief and repentance. Yet this is just the harrowing of the field, to make way for fresh growth from the true vine.

During all this time of searching you will want to be making plans and resolutions, and formulating advice for yourself and others. Don't get attached to these developments and ideas, but don't disdain them. Instead, note them, look at them in the quietness of the heart, and then set them aside. The important thing is to continue steadily, in the presence, in a stillness of your own agendas. Until you have been able to look at your current problem while centered in the love of Christ, you are not likely to see the true value of these plans and ideas. Perhaps they will be very useful, when their time comes; perhaps they are wishful thinking, a premature rushing to closure. Nothing of value will be lost, in the Lord's working in you, if you keep your eye towards his peace and stillness inwardly.

At some point, after a time at the center, you will find that you can, with little or no inner turmoil, look at the fault or grief or dilemma that is the aim of your current exercise. At that moment, when your peace is not shattered by the contemplation of this thing and its meanings, your freedom is begun. Now you can see how to live without it, or overcome it, or account for it in the future, so that you are not its slave any more. Now perhaps your plans and arrangements and resolutions will come in handy, and help you in keeping to the lessons you've learned, when you put them to the test of practice.

When you have experienced the process I have just described, you will discover that the sense of confidence, of foundation, that comes with even a small advance towards the light, is extraordinarily nourishing. If you reflect on it, you will find that you have learned more than one lesson. You will be able to see better how darkness had some hold on you, and the nature of your bondage. You will also see how the light provides the workshop and the tools for removing those bonds, in a way that does not treat each issue separately, but helps you see how all parts of you are interrelated and integrated. So, the solutions that come in that workshop are not patches which can tear away under stress, but form part of a consistent fabric which can contain a measure of life a little larger than before:

> No man putteth a piece of new cloth unto an old garment, for that which is put in to fill it up taketh from the garment, and the rent is made worse. Neither do men put new wine into old bottles; else the bottles break, and the wine runneth out, and the bottles perish; but they put new wine into new bottles, and both are preserved. (Mt 9:16–17)

This process I have described is at the heart of what it is to live in the cross, and it is a place of rejoicing and creation, because you pass through death to a newness of life, and in your own measure and sphere participate in the drama of salvation whose great signs are Calvary and the empty tomb. In this experience, and the making sense of it, every part is of instruction to the minister, because it gives insight into motives, needs, dilemmas, and defeats. It provides a way to interpret and empathize with others' stories, and to take refreshment and courage from their successes and discoveries. It sharpens our understanding of the ways we can be confused or deluded by the many voices that affect us, internally and from our culture and social connections. Finally, it helps us understand how the power of God is the key that unlocks, and how little and yet how necessary are one's own efforts in collaborating with it. With the fresh understanding gained in the school of Christ, you have a keener perception of where that of God may be found in yourself and others, and a renewed eagerness to seek it and stand in it. More than anything else, this is the school in which the minister learns and experiences a transformation of understanding, of perception, and increasingly of enactment.

> While I silently ponder on that change wrought in me, I find no language equal to it, nor any means to convey to another a clear idea of it. I looked upon the works of God in this visible creation and an awfulness covered me; my heart was tender and often contrite, and a universal love to my fellow creatures increased in me. This will be understood by such who have trodden in the same path. Some glances of real beauty may be seen in their faces who dwell in true meekness. There is a harmony in the sound of that voice to which divine love gives utterance, and some appearance of right order in their temper and conduct whose passions are fully regulated. Yet all these do not fully show forth that inward life to such who have not felt it. (Woolman 1971, 29)

6

The life cycle of a minister

Samuel Bownas wrote of a minister's passing through the stages of an infant, a youth, and an adult in the ministry (Bownas 1989). It is almost impossible not to have that framework in mind, as we consider growth in the work of the ministry. It carries with it a substantial element of realism—and also provides both hope and guidance to the new minister.

Yet I believe that you will find that you exist to some degree as a beginner, even after substantial length and maturity of service, and this is to be welcomed and cultivated. This is not a matter of false humility, nor of denial of real progress whose recognition is a key element in the development of one's growth in understanding and practice. It is rather an acknowledgement that progress in the service involves exploring a very large inner landscape—in fact, more than one continent lies open before you, with whose territory you must become more and more familiar. As you find new ground in this exploration, you will find a need to reassess what you have learned before, and the tension between new phenomena and previous lessons may be a place of opening and fresh insight.

The first continent is your self, your own soul's dimensions and conditions. More than anything else, your own inward experience with God as you pass through your life is a laboratory and reference library, and the place where the integrity that is essential to your service is developed. Though you are not the measure of all things, yet you have to speak from the life as you can experience it truthfully and in substance: "[that] which we have heard, which we have seen with our eyes, which we have looked upon, and our hands have handled of the Word of life." (1 John: 1)

The second continent to explore is that of other lives. This, too, is an indispensable source of insight and challenge. There is a great gulf between the inward universe of one individual and that of another, but in the unity of the light, as we come to know it more and more, we are instructed both in the precious uniqueness of each person, and the things that are common to all humans. As we allow ourselves to be instructed and rendered more compassionate through our obedience to the spirit of Christ, we draw closer to God's other children.

The third continent to explore is that of culture. In human terms, the gulf between one and another is bridged by the common products and enterprises of society and culture, which then become part of the fabric of ideas within which we interpret ourselves and others. A deep exploration of this cultural matrix is necessary to an understanding of conditions.

The spiritual grounding and progress of ministers of the present day are often very different from those of Samuel Bownas's day. Many of those who speak in our meetings, and exercise leadership, are not really conversant with the scriptures, or with Quaker tradition. They may not yet have developed a robust spiritual practice. Therefore, as they begin to suspect that they may bear extra responsibility for this service, they are drawn into a time of deepening and searching, which in fact often brings them back to scripture and tradition again. Very often as well it draws them into a fresh engagement with the mystery of Christ.

If the meeting community is alert to this kind of motion in its members, then the gift that may be growing tentatively in someone can be welcomed and nurtured into maturity. If the meeting is not aware that the calling to gospel ministry is still being issued by God, to many Friends, or is not aware that it needs care and support, growing as it does in the context of the life of the worshipping group, the gift can be neglected, or go unrecognized, or bear far less fruit than it might otherwise.

Modern unprogramed Friends who experience this traditional calling and longing to be about the work of God often experience great frustration because there seems to be little or no place for ministry as a vocation in the modern Society of Friends. . . . Part of their frustration lies in the fact that we modern Friends value expertise and genius in virtually every field except the spiritual, so that we don't know how to recognize and encourage a person who is spiritually gifted and called to this work. Every generation of Friends, including this one, has had its quota of people who in other cultures might be called budding shamans or seers or medicine men or medicine women. In earlier Quaker eras these budding Quaker shamans were watched over and nurtured and in subtle ways encouraged so that many of them were able to respond to the ever beaconing call to become a sanctified instrument of the Divine Will. (Taber 1996)

In what follows, I will explore some characteristics of three important phases of the life-cycle of a minister: the time during which one recognizes the call, the period of acceptance and apprenticeship, and the situation of one who has moved beyond apprenticeship.

Recognizing the call

Traditionally, Friends moved into a calling to the ministry gradually, and with a period of anxiety or anticipation, sometimes very lengthy. This presentiment that ministry might be called for usually was embedded in a period of increasing religious seriousness, often after a long period of irreligion or troubled conscience. The ministers, looking back, felt they had fallen into indifference about religion, and heedless living, sometimes punctuated by periods of remorse and short-lived commitment to reform. A tension between these two moods might continue over months or years, with one taking precedence over the other in turn, often in reaction to the previous one: a lack of stability or focus might engender a great desire for a more spiritually centered life, while the experience of intense spiritual practice might rouse a desire for a life less under constraint. Gradually, the seeker might come to an understanding of spiritual practice and focus as a path to freedom and fuller life, and the tension would be resolved (in its most acute phase) and a loyalty declared by visible alterations in behavior. As there was a transition into a more faithful life, and the ordering of the Spirit was felt, Friends often reported a suspicion that one outcome of this birthing process might be service in the ministry. Indeed, having such a possibility arise in the course of the search might be a renewed source of anxiety for a while. Ruth Fallows wrote of this process:

> As I was thus brought near to the Lord and his people, he was pleased to shew me that he had further service for me to do, which was to bear a public testimony for his name. But oh! the exercise this brought upon me, for I found self was yet for being pleased, and I was not willing to be counted a fool, and was for being almost any thing so that the Lord would be pleased without this, that I might not become a gazing stock to the world. (Skidmore 2004, 50–51)

Opening one's mouth in meeting was considered to be an awesome event, as it implied that one felt commissioned by the Holy Spirit to bring a word to the people. This was true for anyone who spoke in meeting, however briefly and rarely. It was also frightening, because the beginner was fearful and lacked confidence, and felt that in yielding to duty they would appear foolish—either in the quality of their service, or because the Gospel might appear foolishness (as Paul describes in 1 Cor.) However, the emergence of a sustained gift in the ministry was a momentous event in the life of a meeting, and required considerable care on the part of the community to discern what was happening, and how best to respond. Since God can choose anyone to be a friend or servant—wise or foolish, powerful or weak, respectable or not (1 Cor. 1:26), anyone, however unlikely, might be under divine preparation for service. Speaking in meeting, therefore, might be the first evidence of a commission to the work of the ministry, so it bears watching.

An aside: sometimes the "standard history" of resistance and acceptance of calling to the ministry has been portrayed as almost a pathological peculiarity of the Quietist culture of the eighteenth and nineteenth centuries. Yet I think that the matter looks different if one realizes that a gift in the ministry was considered precious and deserving of careful stewardship. Though it was in some sense seen as a normal part of the life of a meeting, it was also an awesome thing, because the gift means that Peter, Paul, Jonah, Isaiah, Ezekiel, Fox, and others are your colleagues and fellow workers. It was also well known that the gift could sometimes be very inconvenient or even frightening, as well as very satisfying. Because it is precious, other things must make way for it, and you couldn't predict at the outset how intrusive and demanding it might be. The power of the Spirit can be consuming and bewildering; at times, you must just abandon yourself to it, in obedience and hope.

This is still true. God may well make use of you in ways that are not so hard to accommodate in the life you currently know. It may be, though, that God will sometimes (or increasingly) make it your duty to work harder than you are inclined to, make choices that will be hard or surprising, push you in ways that test your emotional, spiritual, or physical strength. If you are really under orders, and not merely moving according to your own designs and desires, then you may well be taken off guard. Just remember that when you hear ministers speak of the challenges and trials they have undergone, you will also hear them speak of the joy and peace they have enjoyed. Do not dismiss this as cold comfort! The joy and the peace are very real.

In modern times, it seems to be rare for someone to have a sense that they are under preparation for gospel ministry, before they are actually engaged in it. As William Taber has written:

> It is almost as if, in the late twentieth century, Bownas's first qualifi-
> cation [of sanctification] does not tend to occur before one speaks
> in meeting, but rather stretches out over a number of years,
> gradually transforming and eventually bringing that person's life
> and spoken ministry to a deeper level. (Bownas 1989, Taber
> introduction, xxii)

It seems also to be the case for many modern Friends that speaking in meeting is part of their preparation, so that engaging in that activity is itself a schooling process of the Spirit, however unaware we are that this is the case. Putting things into publicly uttered words is a way of identifying an increasing seriousness and commitment, and implies an intent to live accordingly. Jonathan Dale writes:

> I was led to minister in ways that called me to a position that I had not yet reached, and then demanded a greater consistency between the words uttered and the life lived. However that ministry spoke to others, it certainly played its part in changing me. (Dale 1996, 37)

This is reminiscent of my own experience. I had been attending meeting for perhaps five years, with increasing commitment, and during that time found myself among those who spoke in meeting several times a year. More seasoned Friends would sometimes say a quiet word of encouragement to me, which was gratifying and reassuring, as my standing up was always attended with a feeling of turmoil and risk, which grew in part of out of my understanding that worship is a serious matter, and if God is really directing our worship, it is a fearsome thing to offer one's words as evidence of divine activity.

Friends my own age, who were also coming into increasing service in the meeting's affairs, were in the habit of talking about meeting events, and we naturally discussed the meeting for worship, as well. We gave each other comments and advice, explored why we were moved by some people's ministry and not others on a particular day, chewed over how each of us could serve, and what we seemed to be good at. We named gifts that we saw in each other.

My friends' reflection of what they saw developing in me made me wonder—could I see in myself what they were seeing? What might be the roots of it? If they were right, what difference should it make in my life? The words I was saying challenged me to greater integrity, but so did my friends' encouragement of my service; and so did mistakes and rebukes. Our conversations about each other's gifts and growth made more of our inner lives accessible for reflection and cultivation. I rejoiced when I received inward or outward guidance that helped me forward, but I felt the need of more experienced companions, as well.

I did not know of any Friends in my community to whom I could talk, even if I had been able to formulate the questions I was feeling. It was at this point that I started reading journals, branching out from Fox and Woolman to Bownas and beyond, and found some real solace in the lives and experiences of these dedicated men and women. It also happened that Darcy Drayton and I spent a few days visiting at the parsonage of Durham (Maine) Meeting with Ralph Greene. In conversation one evening, when I described to him my growing sense of responsibility, he said, "Look, what you're dealing with is a call to the ministry, don't you see? You need to think about that."

Since this was not the way that Quakers that I knew talked I meditated on Ralph's challenge in secret for a long time, struggling to figure out how that "calling," so clearly a part of previous periods of Quakerism, could take any acceptable shape in the Religious Society of Friends I knew. I sat with it in meeting, and continued for a while to feel isolated.

Yet once I was able to accept the nature of the challenge, not only was I able to give coherence to my own inner spiritual life, but my eyes were sharpened to see others who were actually exploring the same question. I found living teachers in unexpected places, and other beginners like myself, just coming into an acceptance of the concern. We helped each other along. The sort of clarity that came as I was able to identify the service I felt called to is one evidence that a concern has been identified and accepted. This clarity, in turn, is also the beginning place of many inquiries.

The encouragement of others, both the more experienced Friends, and those who were younger in their Quaker lives, was instructive, and encouraging. We need to hear that we have been helpful, so that our discernment is not too self-referential. It is true, however, that "feedback" can also cause different problems if it plays into insecurities or tendencies to inflation. Insecurity can make us fearful of following our

guide, but when combined with encouragement can contribute to the construction of protective illusions, and tempt
us to think of our ministry as personal property, or a matter of
more or less effective performance. John Griffith writes of his
experience in youth, when encouragement from his friends
led him to move too fast, and believe he had made more
progress in the spiritual life (out of which ministry grows)
than he actually had:

> Many young well-minded people, and some others of little expe-
> rience, seemed to admire my gift, and would sometimes speak
> highly of it, which they did not always forbear in my hearing. But
> oh how dangerous this is, if delighted in by ministers! It may be
> justly compared to poison, which will soon destroy the pure
> innocent life. My judgment was against it; yet I found something
> in me, that seemed to have no aversion thereunto, but rather
> inclined to hearken to it, yet not with full approbation. The
> same thing in me would want to know, what such and such, who
> were in much esteem for experience and wisdom, thought of
> me. I sometimes imagined such looked shy upon me, which
> would much cast me down; all which, being from a root or fibre
> of self, I found was for judgment, and must die upon the cross,
> before I was fit to be trusted with any great store of gospel treas-
> ure. I begun [sic] also to take rather too much delight myself in
> the gift . . . I have reason to think, that solid friends, observing
> my large growth in the top, with spreading branches, were in
> fear of my downfall, in case of a storm. However, in the midst of
> my high career, the Lord was pleased to take away from me, for a
> time, that which he had given me, viz., the gift of ministry, and
> with it all sensible comforts of the spirit. ... In this doleful state of
> mind, I was grievously beset and tempted by the false prophet . . .
> to keep up my credit in the ministry, by continuing in my pub-
> lick [sic] appearances. (Griffith 1779, 29)

Encouragement and guidance from admired Friends can
have a similar effect of letting us think we have discovered
more than we have. Catherine Phillips wrote of going to a
large public meeting early in her service, and of the careful
way more experienced ministers responded to her:

> It was attended by many valuable experienced ministers, who were
> careful of laying hands suddenly upon me, although I had good

reason to believe that the most weighty of them loved me; but were fearful of hurting me by discovering too much of their approbation or affection; which some minds, in the infancy of religious experience, have not been able to hear. (Skidmore 2004, 70)

We need to listen to our Friends, but always come back to God, to the quiet place where we feel free to be honest, regardless for the moment of our fears, hopes, plans, and impulses.

Wherefore let your food be in the life of what you know, and in the power of obedience rejoice, and not in what you know, but cannot live, for the life is the bread for your souls, which crucifies the flesh, and confounds that which runs before the cross. (Nayler, in Drayton 1994, 69)

Apprenticeship

Not many people have the chance to experience the process of being an apprentice in a craft, in the old-fashioned sense, though apprenticeships are in fact common enough, in unusual guise. I am happy that I have seen it up close in several forms, and it is worth stopping for a moment to draw some lessons from those experiences which also apply to the apprenticeship in the gospel ministry. My experiences with apprenticeship have included both a "white collar" experience (graduate study in a science), and also craft work (watching my father undertake apprenticeship as a piano tuner in middle age, and myself in informal apprenticeships in blacksmithing and lobster fishing).

When you are an apprentice, the first thing that bears upon you is the desire to become a competent practitioner of the craft, eventually maybe even a master. You have acknowledged that you want to really be the best workman you can be. This awareness in itself has far-reaching effects. As one Friend said to me, when describing how his meeting's acknowledgment of his gift affected him: "I couldn't believe it. The whole world suddenly looked different somehow."

Second, you gain real insight, a concrete feeling, about the range of things to be learned on the path to mastery—all the things you need to learn, and maybe don't see how to. There are many small, simple things which are needed, before you can try the more obviously rewarding acts. As an apprentice blacksmith, for example, you need to learn quite a lot about the building, shaping, and maintenance of the fire in the forge, and how different sorts of fires relate to different kinds of work. Of course, this means a lot of experience with smoke, steam, and coal dust, a lot of metal not heated enough, a lot of welds not completed: simple stuff, but all in the service of the craft or art, the "higher" work you seek to learn.

Third, you learn how competence can take many different forms. Personal styles and limitations enter in, and also the accidents of one's history—the people you've been able to watch, the guidance or help you've received, the challenges or opportunities that have come your way. You also start to see how, even as you learn the basics, your own practice has to emerge.

Fourth, you learn how to accept criticism, whether ill-natured or well-intended. In fact, I think a real test of your condition with regard to a concern is, can you receive rebuke or advice mildly and judiciously? This does not mean that you need to accept the other person's assessment, or agree with their view point. Yet it is important to acknowledge that they are very likely seeking your good or that of the meeting, even if it does not feel like that to you, and defensiveness in the face of hard questions is a strong piece of evidence that ego is involved to an inappropriate degree. This is a danger sign!

Finally, most "masters" have a keen sense of what else they have to learn. Part of apprenticeship, one of the surprising doorways to the wisdom of the craft, is learning what to do with not-knowing.

These kinds of lessons are likely to arise when you enter into an apprenticeship in the gospel ministry. Nowadays, especially in unprogrammed meetings, we take a long time to realize or even bring ourselves to admit that we are called to have a concern for the gospel ministry, and most people have little sense that it is a work in which one can—should—grow more capable over time. The language for talking about it is not usual with us, we don't see others around who admit to having travelled different distances along that road, meetings don't usually name the gift that is stirring in us—many reasons! However, at the moment when you come to see that this is one of the organizing concerns in your life, then you can actually begin your apprenticeship. This is a time of joy, even exhilaration, and also a time for care. When we start to be intentional about service, we are prey to many kinds of anxieties about performance and adequacy. We may also (perhaps because of such anxieties) be defensive, assertive, or prideful, becoming hardened when we should be growing more open and fearless. We are tempted also to compare ourselves to others.

During this time, it is good to look around for others who may be under the same concern in their own way. A good place to begin is with journals and other written accounts, because they are at some distance of time and culture, and the differences between your experience and theirs are stimulating of perspective and reflection. Furthermore, their stories, however filtered, allow you to think about the way lives unfold under the influence of a long-term concern, from the tender beginnings through decades of service.

The most important thing, however, is to practice more carefully than you might have been practicing previously—going to meeting for worship regularly, attending meetings for business, attending committee meetings and so on. These accustomed activities will start to feel different under the consciousness of the concern for the ministry, because they will seem linked by the opportunities with God that they offer—and sometimes do not deliver. On the other hand, you will come to your meetings, committees, workshops, etc., in a more centered and observant frame of mind, more alert and teachable.

This is also a good time to visit other meetings, to read new things, to listen carefully to the ministry in meeting, to consider the characteristics of experienced Friends, and to reflect on any ministry you may be moved to offer. Your service is to

Friends (and perhaps others) right now, and so it is good to set yourself the task of listening and observing afresh, to see as well as you can what are the concerns, the opportunities, the limits, and the strengths of modern Quakerism.

Most especially, it is important to find some Friend or Friends with whom you can talk about your sense of calling. In this way, you will start to understand the lessons you need to learn, the different kinds of gifts that can be used in ministry, the shape that the daily watch may take.

During this time, your consciousness of a desire for service, and opening way to it, will make you careful to adjust your life so as not to dishonor the ministry that you claim to participate in. You will start to learn both the rewards, and also the kinds of adversity that come from self-criticism, or from the inner weather of the spirit, and our wavering faithfulness. You will also find your eye and heart sharpened to feel the way you are chained and bound by fears, bad habits, cultural detriments: to use traditional language, you feel how you need to come under the cross, if you are to be any use at all to the Lord who seems to be calling you.

Sometimes things will seem easy and straightforward; sometimes rather the opposite. Be patient, and return patiently to the Lord for guidance, and also support. Bownas wrote of this time in his own life:

> The poverty of my spirit was so exceedingly great and bitter that I could scarcely bear it, but cried out loud, which so surprised my companion that he, being on foot, he feared it would be too hard for me, for I complained that I was deceived or mistaken; because, while I was in my master's work, I rarely by day or night was without some degree of Divine virtue upon my mind, but now I could feel nothing but the bitterness of death and darkness; all comfort was hid from me for a time, and I was baptized into death indeed. As we went along, I said to Isaac with a vehemence of spirit: "Oh! that I was in my master's work again, and favored with my former enjoyments of Divine life, how acceptable it would be!

> The Lord let me see his kindness to lead me through that state of poverty, which was of great service to qualify me to speak to others in the like condition, and that trials of sundry kinds were

for my improvement and good, tending to my establishment in the true root of a Divine and spiritual ministry; and the doctrine of our Saviour and his apostle did much comfort me, so that I became, in the opinion of several, an able minister, although but short, seldom standing a quarter of an hour. But alas! I have seen since that I was but a mere babe in the work. (Bownas 1839, 5)

It is during your apprenticeship, the onset of intentionality, that you will start to think about how to serve more effectively. As you read the journals or speak with other ministers, you will find it compelling to understand the discipline of waiting for the fresh calling of the Spirit before acting, and also the simple disciplines of competent performance: about being careful to be audible, clear, and simple in delivery, to be diligent and faithful, and so on.

It becomes increasingly important as your service continues to seek out a spiritual friend or friends—someone with whom to practice complete honesty and simplicity in telling the story of your current experience and questions, opportunities and roadblocks. In such a friendship, though, the first priority should be shared worship, time spent in God's presence together. This rootedness in the ardent and peaceable spirit of Christ will help counteract a tendency to close in, to become overly preoccupied with self, or too ethereal, to lose perspective and hence stop learning.

It seems especially important for the person experiencing the call to ministry to find a spiritual friend or mentor, someone with whom it is possible to sit in deep silence before God as well as to stay accountable and to test leadings, and to explore what it means to live on the razor's edge of ministry. Ideally, this person would be a member of the local worship and ministry group, but don't give up if you can not find such a person there; there may be someone else in the meeting, or that person may exist in a nearby meeting, or you may have to seek someone who lives a hundred miles away. But a right spiritual friend is somewhere to be found for every seeker and for every person who feels called into ministry. Actually, as one becomes more experienced, opportunities for finding spiritual friends and spiritual peers tend to increase, so that one called to ministry gradually finds oneself discovering a network of kindred souls, with increasing opportunities for "opportunities." It is as if those called to ministry are often drawn to opportunities with many people, as if we become a part of a vast process of cross-fertilization of the Spirit throughout the entire Society of Friends, and far beyond. (Taber 1996)

In previous times, when Friends assumed that some would be particularly called into the gospel ministry, they were forthright about craftsmanlike considerations, such as the proper procedure for getting a travel minute, and observing matters of personal style and presentation that may actually hinder your simple, direct, and honest testimony. One of the charms of Samuel Bownas' reflections is his willingness to consider pretty mundane issues, in order to be a good workman. For example, in the following passage from his journal, he addresses many problems that arise for most people who speak in meeting and question whether they have done it appropriately:

> I found I often hurt myself by speaking too fast and too loud . . . but when I felt my heart filled with the power of Divine love, I was apt to forget myself and break out. I found it proper therefore to stop, and make a short pause, with secret prayer for preservation, and that I would be supplied with matter and power, that might do the hearers good. Thus I went on, and grew sensibly in experience and judgment, and became in some small degree skillful in dividing the word. I had been straitened in my mind respecting searching the scriptures, lest I should be tempted thereby to lean upon them, and by gathering either manna or sticks on the Sabbath-day, death would ensue. But at last I had freedom to examine the text, and to consider where the strength of the argument lay; both before and after the words I had repeated. By this I saw that I was often very defective, in not laying hold of the most suitable part to confirm the subject or matter I was upon, and this conduct did me great service. Another difficulty stood in my way, which was this: some former openings would come up, which I durst not meddle with, lest by so doing I should become formal, and lose that Divine spring which I had always depended upon; but the Lord was pleased to show me, that old matter, opened in new life, was

always new, and that it was the renewings of the spirit alone which made it new; and that the principal thing I was to guard against was, not to endeavour to bring in old openings in my own will, without the aid of the spirit and that if I stood single and resigned to the Divine will, I should be preserved from errors of this nature (Bownas 1839, 7).

After some years

After living with this commitment to service, and gaining some experience with acting out of this orientation, you will find (to your surprise, perhaps) that you have in fact learned much. Your experience will give rise to some challenges not felt before, as well as a sense of maturity and confidence in the Lord's reliable guidance. You will also have begun to learn the many ways that guidance can come, and how a growing sense of integration is one of its telltale signs. William Taber, in writing about this growth of discernment, nicely connects the growth of discernment about a particular act of ministry with the growing acquaintance with God's guiding voice, and the increased awareness of it throughout the day:

> Many generations of experienced Quaker ministers have spoken of learning to attend to the inward motion, sometimes described as the "still small voice." In the beginning it can be so subtle and delicate as it first rises up through the clear pool of consciousness that it certainly does not seem like a motion or a voice. It is simply a quiet knowing with no fireworks, so that it can easily be confused with other thoughts and impulses if we are not attentive. Sometimes, the Spirit pushes the inward motion up through the layers of consciousness so that we can not ignore it, and the Spirit overcomes our resistance to it by causing us to quake, or at least to cause rapid breathing and heart beat, which are often regarded as the signs that one must speak in meeting.
>
> But, as we become experienced in recognizing and responding to the inward motion, the Spirit does not need to expend so much energy on us; we become more able to discern the power of the Divine Urgency of the true inward motion and to discern which other thoughts and "motions"—no matter how good and worthy—are to be left alone, or at least not be spoken as ministry.

Of course, the inward motion, or the inward knowing which is
another way of describing the guidance of the Holy Spirit, is not
just an esoteric skill for those who speak in our meetings.
Quakerism is about, among other things, the fact that this guidance through the inward motion is available to every one of us,
in the daily affairs of our lives, as well as our special ministry in
family, meeting community, and world to which each of us is
called. (Taber 1996)

You will have learned a lot about what you are called to do,
the kinds of service you are gifted for, your personal "style" of
ministry. As part of this, you will have gone through several
experiences of specific events, and gained some perspective
on the "typical" course that may be expected. For example,
several times you may have felt a calling to travel to some
place or undertake some specific concern, gone to the meeting with a request for a travel minute or other endorsement,
and carried through the discernment process. Then you will
have undertaken the visit or task, and returned the minute—
and learned over time how these rhythms can include deep
periods of doubt and frustration, or a dawning understanding, once you've begun, of what the nature of the concern
really was, what you needed to learn by doing it, as well as
what you might actually have to offer to the people you are
sent to. You will have gained some experience with unexpected blessings, insights, inspirations, and discouragements.

By now, you should also be feeling both confidence that God
can be relied upon, and that you have learned how to be reliable in listening, in acting or keeping still, as led. One way to
say this is, you will have gained some freedom from fear, including the fear of being wrong or foolish, and from many preconceptions about the ministry. You will perhaps feel secure in the
service, and also more teachable and committed to gratitude
for your own blessings, and for the growth and life in others.

As part of this learning, you will no doubt have been
advised several times about mistakes you have made, places
you've made people uncomfortable, blind spots or bad habits
that interfere with your contribution to the life of the Society.

If you have been able to stay low enough to come through these challenges with meekness, and a singleness of purpose to be faithful, your openness and firmness both will be instructive and nourishing to yourself and your community.

Perhaps most important, you will have learned ways in which to speak to others from time to time about their service, speaking even difficult things in love, in a tone that is direct but conveys also your support for their growth and gifts. For my own part, I have found that I have more and more taken joy in the times when I have been able to speak encouragement to others in various kinds of service, to help them forward in times of doubt or struggle. I have been restrained, I trust, from an over-eagerness to give advice: the joy is not in being an authority, but in being able to feel others' conditions sympathetically but not sentimentally, and make some contribution to their way forward.

Finally, the distance you've travelled, and the things you've learned from your work should be bringing you to a deeper sensitivity, both to the sorrow and darkness in the world, and the great joy that there is, so that you can say with George Fox that you see the ocean of darkness and death, and yet the ocean of light and life flowing over it. Your real acquaintance with the night makes your testimony of joy more precious.

Praying for continued growth

There are, of course, issues to confront with growing experience.

First and foremost is a loss of keenness, of real availability to the Spirit. Depending on how you enact it, the ministry can be an unobtrusive career, and therefore you can become by degrees habitual and in a sense lifeless in the concern. You will have confronted some dilemmas about your own gifts and limitations. You will perhaps have encountered some opposition or discomfort within your meeting, and reached some accommodation. You will have made some adjustments so as to continue securing your livelihood, while not quite abandoning your ministry. In short, you will have moved to a place of comfort.

Sometimes, a place of stability is achieved because you have kept the balance in a dynamic system, and are moment to moment sensing the pull of one force or another threatening to dislodge you, and yet able to compensate. On the other hand, you may be stable because you are at a point where there is no risk. A living prayer life is the most reliable avenue to being able to tell the difference between good balance and stagnation, and so it is valuable to make sure that as part of your "system" you build in times when you are regularly forced out of your normal rounds—making an annual retreat, for example, or arranging to have periodic meetings with a spiritual friend whom you have asked to challenge you from time to time. Meeting with other Friends in the ministry can play the same role, if the conversations sometimes explore the questions: Are we being faithful and open to new paths of service? Are we learning? Are we feeling challenged? However still and small the voice of the Lord in our experience, you may need to remind yourself to wait a little longer until you find again the taste of dimensionless mystery.

Perhaps at times like this it is good to explore a bit, to find things you are uncomfortable about, and understand why. Someone in the meeting is raising an issue you have no patience for, perhaps. There are developments in society or politics that make you irritated or depressed or confused. A good exercise is to take a month and read critically through a couple of Friends periodicals of differing styles (for example *Friends Journal* and *Quaker Life*), and really make yourself confront and debate (inwardly) with the authors, while also asking yourself what of their opinions is true but uncomfortable.

The point is not stimulation, really, however, but an active mode of seeking one's boundaries and growing edges. Some people do this habitually, and they are wonderfully alive. You may not have achieved that state yet, as most of us have not. This kind of intentional search is a specific way to pray for fresh growth.

In the end, however, the goal is to keep as simple, as available, and as little self-assertive as possible. This may seem to contradict the idea of growth in maturity and assurance in the concern for gospel ministry, but it is actually integral to it. If your growing experience does not bear fruit in joy, as well as humility, sensitivity, and a confidence in God's secret work, then it is important to ask whether you are coming to rely upon yourself, and value yourself, more than is healthy. If so, you are in good company, since almost all ministers who've ever recorded their experiences have reported such a tendency. Once being alerted, however, turn back to God's presence, and feel towards the simple, childlike Spirit, where resides the power you really wish to serve.

> [A]s you become faithful thereto, you will feel the fruit of that Holy One springing in you, moving to be brought forth in you towards God and man, your faith will grow, and prayers with strong cries to the Father; as the Spirit sees your wants, your love will spring and move in you, and bring forth towards God and man upon all occasions; which if you willingly serve in its smallest motion, it will increase, but if you quench it in its movings, and refuse to bring it forth, it will wither and dry in you, not being exercised.
>
> And it is the like of gentleness, meekness, patience, and all other virtues which are of a springing and spreading nature, where they are not quenched, but suffered to come forth to His praise in His will and time, who is the Begetter thereof, and to the comfort of His own Seed, and cross to the world: And if you be faithful daily to offer up your body as a sacrifice, to bring forth His image, name, and power before His enemies, then what He moves you to bring forth shall be your inheritance, and will daily increase with using; but if you will not give up for His name[']s sake, but would hold the treasure, and escape the reproach, then will it be taken from you, and given to him who will yield the Lord of the vineyard His fruit in due season; for that which the Father freely begets, He will have freely brought forth, that the shining thereof in the dark world may praise Him. (Nayler, in Drayton 1994, 56)

Does the concern continue?

There is no sense that gospel ministry is a "lifetime appointment." By thinking of a calling to ministry as a concern, we are enabled periodically to ask the question, does the concern continue with me? Is it still alive, or should I lay it down?

> More than once in my own history I have been on the point of resigning my position as a recorded minister; not from any doubt as to my original call, nor on account of any apprehended disunity with my service, but because I felt it so desirable that the Friends of my monthly meeting should have a definite opportunity of reconsidering their judgment after a few years' observation. If their approval had been reaffirmed, it would have afforded me encouragement (at times greatly needed) to persevere in the work. If otherwise, it would have enabled me to lay down with a clear conscience a responsibility which often seemed too great to bear. (Dymond 1892, 49–50)

I believe that it is important to keep this question alive, and revisit it from time to time. I make a point of addressing it explicitly in reporting to my meeting every year (see appendix 2), because an honest consideration of this question helps keep me mindful that I should be seeking to serve, and to act in this particular kind of service under a fresh sense of divine requirement. Making it explicit also gives my meeting an opportunity to comment upon it. There are times when, like Dymond, I would feel a real sense of relief at being released from this focus, either because of fatigue, or a sense of inadequacy, or discouragement.

Yet when a time of dryness or a sense of uselessness comes, and you consider that perhaps you should lay down the concern, it is important to get some distance from the feelings of the moment, and not be too hasty to set aside a gift still being given. It is good to consider this carefully, and in consultation both with your meeting (under some circumstances) and perhaps first with other, experienced ministers, because the life of this concern can have seasons of rest or abeyance, arising from many different causes; and also because the identification of the concern rests in part on your own discernment, and in part on that of the community.

It may be because you have gone through a period in which unwittingly you have relaxed your daily watch. This will dull your inward alertness, and can bring on a sense of cool-ness and distance from the things of the Spirit, which will sap one's usefulness. If this is continued too long, it can lead to significant disaffection and, in effect, the loss of the gift, sapped by a loss of love and engagement. This is something that all Friends are vulnerable to, of course, and it is especially valuable for ministers to understand this. In a way, the issue is more poignant, or more clearly drawn, since the minister is following a vocation to service, while also for the most part needing to seek a livelihood and otherwise engage in domes-tic and professional activities. It is a gift that a concerned Friend can give others, to acquire and maintain the discipline needed to balance the many demands of "temporal" and "spiritual," and in this way grow in an understanding of the unity between the two. The challenge of temporary coldness has been known from the beginning of our Society. Here is James Nayler advising on this problem:

> So when you feel your way darkened, or affections grow cold towards heaven, then take heed with all diligence in the pure light to search, for your enemy has got some entrance, which by faithful and patient waiting in the light you will come to see. . . . Wherefore, that which you have received of the Holy One, His Unction, hold fast till He come, and with it stand armed against whatever would enter, to lead out to any outward observations; but with all diligence observe that which you have of His in spirit, which the adversary seeks so much to draw you forth from, lest you should increase your Lord's money, and herein you maintain your daily watch, and war with that you have of life and power, and not with that you have not: So are you faithful stewards, and are accepted in what you have, and not in what you have not. (Nayler, in Drayton 1994, 68)

Again, you may be in a time of quiet because of personal challenges that are deeply disturbing, and require much spiri-tual work of you—healing or growth. A death in the family, a personal illness, the loss of a job, trouble in the meeting, or sim-ple fatigue—so many things may burden us, and at times like this it may well be important to be quiet, and take the time of retirement you need. After all, your discernment will likely be impaired, and the springs of gratitude and confidence in God may well be hard to find. During such times, maintain your practice of retirement and prayer, and as part of that be sure to stay available, and willing to serve when the time comes.

In this connection, I have often thought about an incident from the life of John Stephenson Rowntree, a minister in Yorkshire in the nineteenth century, and uncle of John Wilhelm Rowntree. A loved and diligent minister, in early middle life he lost his beloved wife, leaving behind him and their children in grief. His biographers write:

> As each day brought an added realisation of change and loss, felt with such keenness, also on his children's account, his sensitive heart was torn not with grief only, but with the pangs of a questioning that tested the very foundations of his faith. . . . A cousin writes it was some time after this great bereavement before his voice was again heard in the ministry. He rose first with the question of the prisoner in Machaerus, "Art thou he that shall come, or look we for another?" (Doncaster 1908, 35)

Rowntree had been challenged by his grief to examine his faith, and determine if he could honestly speak in instruction and exhortation. Clearly, the sense of responsibility to minister had not left him, but his inward condition required healing and clarification, if he was to speak under the Spirit's leading, and not merely because it was expected of him.

Finally, you may actually be led into silence because it is the lesson you need to learn, and also to teach. If you are familiar with Quaker journals, you have read many instances in which the minister feels called to "set an example of silence," because she felt the meeting was too expectantly waiting for words. Yet again, we may need to be silent because we have become comfortable with speaking, feel much satisfaction in our service in that line, and need to recalibrate ourselves, recentering on the inward teacher, and getting away from too much reliance on our ideas, reading, experience, opinions, gifts of expression.

Catherine Phillips describes her experience of a time of learning silence, in terms that many of her contemporaries did, as they came through searching times to the same realization:

I was stripped of that strength wherewith the Almighty had been pleased to clothe me . . . insomuch that I was ready to doubt of all that I had known, and call in question my commission to minister, and . . . [I was] baptized into a cloud of darkness. This dispensation I afterwards saw to be useful . . . for therein I forgot all my former services, was emptied of all self-sufficiency, and became weak and depending as when I first engaged in the weighty service of ministry; and it lives in my experience, that thus the Lord will deal with his servants, for their preservation, that they may dwell in a continual sense, that the excellency is of Him; from whom proceeds wisdom, power, light, utterance, peace, and every good gift. (Skidmore 2004, 71)

In this time of outward inactivity, we may come to feel an intensified focus on prayer for the state of the meeting, and for the appearance there of fresh signs of growth and development—in witness, in a strengthened sense of personal acquaintance with God, in ministry in worship, in forgiveness, or new commitment to the community. In such times, we are able to feel more vividly the currents of life moving within the meeting, and renew the simplicity of our hearts.

William Taber often described a time in his life when he was silenced, after a period of growing freedom and effectiveness in the meeting. During this time, he continued to recognize when the meeting needed a message, and what the message was, but he felt a "stop" in the way of his offering it. He came to understand that he was being taught about the most important ministry of all, "the ministry of secret, silent radiation of God's love to all who are present in the meeting." (Abbott and Parsons 2004, 114) There were Friends who might never speak in meeting, might not be seen as leaders or "weighty," whose gift to the meeting was their steady centeredness in love. "When I had fully learned this, and had begun to discover how to become a radiator myself, I could again speak in meeting, with the same power as before."

These women and men would not have understood if I had complimented them on being masters of the Quaker technology of shifting levels of consciousness and the secret of prayerful presence. In fact, they would probably have been embarrassed and confused by my language. But, with all their humility, they were exercising the technology with great skill in a way which made it possible for fools like me to speak. . . . Fortunate is that meeting which has such inconspicuous and silent, radiating souls within its midst, for their faithful presence helps not only to raise up a living spoken ministry, but also to encourage the gathered and covered quality of the worship out of which the ministry flows. And fortunate is that meeting in which those who speak are, at the same time, also practitioners of the invisible and silent ministry. (Taber 1996)

When I first experienced such times of schooling silence, it caused me some confusion and anxiety, because I had only recently accepted the calling to ministry. What could it mean that my inward commitment was followed, not by an increase of service, but a diminishment? Eventually, I realized that, while silent, I was feeling no rebuke or sense of having erred. Rather, I recognized a strong need to study, to listen to others, and to learn better how to pray, both privately and in the meeting. It was as if I was rewarded for my commitment by a vision of how much a beginner I was, and by guidance into the next lessons that I needed to learn. Looking back, I can see that I was drawn into a new period of preparation and qualification for a more public service, but saved from any presumption that I knew "my business." It isn't my business, after all, it's God's; yet in this I found confidence. Thanks to this preparation, I was then able to profit from the stories told in the journals, and by living Friends, about such experiences. I find now that I am even cheered by such times of quiet— even when they are outwardly inconvenient.

Finally, just as others have written, I have come to be a little freer from attachment to the gift, thanks to these times of quiet. Being taught to listen more carefully to the sources of real life and power in the meeting, I understand better how the ministry "fits" in the dynamic of a healthy meeting, and the value and limits of my own passing contribution. I know that if a time comes when I ask, "Am I to lay down this concern?" and the answer is "Yes," I will be able to hear it in peace.

7

The minister's devotional life[6]

The largest portion of the labor entailed by a concern for the ministry is primarily enacted in private, rather than in the outward events where the gift may be exercised. Every Friend is admonished to find a time of quiet retirement daily, and to study the scriptures and other devotional literature regularly. But if you are led into a concern gospel ministry, you need even more to pay attention to your devotional life. The reason is that this time is an important part of your school and your laboratory. It is here that you wait to be instructed by the Lord, both in expectant waiting, and in reflection upon the material of your experience and your reading.

Earlier I made the point that "a living ministry begets a living people." Here I wish to emphasize that a *living* ministry is a *listening* ministry. Your growth in your gift should be accompanied by a growing ability and desire to listen for the life of the Spirit in events, stories, people—both from the present and from the past. In this chapter and the several following, I address several aspects of this listening: study, prayer, scripture, and Friends tradition.

Study and writing

It is worth spending a little time on the subject of reading and study, because Friends have always asserted that right ministry is not a matter of intellectual accomplishments. You are not expected to learn ancient languages, read abstruse texts, and keep up with current developments in philosophy and theology. However, concerned Friends in every age, from the time of Fox down to the present, have found that study of some kind becomes an important part of their discipline and

[6] I here borrow the title of a valuable little address by Geoffrey Nuttall, from which any Friend may profit. Full citation found in the bibliography.

growth. Reading helps amplify one's personal scope, sets people, issues, and events in context, feeds the search for the causes of things, reminds us of the complexities of life and the universe. Furthermore, it is often valuable to know what has been written and said on the topics of special concern to you, whether it is prayer, social action, doctrine, history, or whatever. Since the service of gospel ministry is in part a service of words and thought, your service may well be strengthened by systematic encounter with others' ideas and formulations, Quaker and otherwise. The main thing is that whether you study widely or not, all your reading should be informed or guided by your commitment to service, and your desire for the good of souls.

By this, I do not mean at all that the study and reflection are intended as preparation of sermons to be delivered—this is a point widely addressed in books and advices already. I will only add here, that if you read and study, and do it in a reflective way, and especially if you keep a journal or other notebook as an aid to the reflection and as a learning tool, you will often find yourself constructing inward discourses on the basis of passages or ideas that capture your attention. This is so natural to our minds, that one may want to defend it as reasonable and harmless, as long as the material is not unloaded before it is really called for. Indeed, decisions in this regard are made more complicated by the habit of some ministering Friends, for example Rufus Jones, of noting down important insights or lines of thought and reviewing them from time to time, so that sermons in a sense grow organically around these kernels. In terms of meditation and deep consideration of ideas or issues, there is much to recommend this. This seemed especially attractive at a time in Quakerism when a renewal of the "teaching ministry" was one of the most frequently voiced needs, and it was felt that rightly prepared Friends were too inclined to stay silent.

Yet it is my experience that if one keeps this kind of encapsulated notes, sermon-kernels, it is harder to judge when one is really called to speak *this* message to *these* people at *this* moment, as distinct from a time when a good thought has ripened until it is ready for dispersal. Therefore, if you are a person who likes to take notes, organize your reading, and so on, your discipline before and during meeting must include additional care to set such prepared material aside, and seek in real openness for a sense of present need. Note well, that if, as you ask yourself about this, the answer is always "Oh, go ahead!" it may well be that you are answering to your own satisfaction rather than waiting for real guidance.

This is not a new problem. Concerned Friends have always found their minds engaged in trains of ideas and images that feel as though they are intended for use in the ministry. Here is John Conran, an Irish Friend (1739–1827), describing his experience:

> In managing my outward business, in the garden and fields by myself, I sometimes have felt a living language in my heart as if I were addressing an assembly of people, and it used to begin so imperceptibly in me, that it would be moving some minutes before I would turn my attention to it, and when I did, it increased so much as to bubble up like a spring, and break me into tears, and left a sweet savor and comfort behind. These were I believe only the first-fruits of the Spirit, and the ministration of preparation for the important work of the ministry, and which I fear some have taken for the work itself. (Conran 1877, 33–4)

Such experiences are not uncommonly reported in the journals, and the authors are unanimous in their sense that such openings are serviceable, provided one never used the material so assembled just because it was cogent and instructive. It was to be set aside, in one's mind or in writing, with a prayer that it enrich one's preparation, and go into the storehouse from which the good servant draws good things new and old to share when the real need arises, and the Master directs. Nothing is ever wasted.

I should add further that when you are in a period of concentrated service, as in an extended visit in the ministry among a series of meetings, your mind may rightly be so thoroughly engaged and dedicated during that time, that your meditations are entwined with your concern for the people being visited more or less constantly. You still need to wait until a real call comes. In your discernment, be open to the possibility that you may be used in ways which you have not been while at home in your own meeting, or at times when you are following a concern in a less concentrated fashion. Job Scott reports how in his travels in the ministry, his mind was engaged with meetings he was about to visit for hours ahead of time, as though he had already entered the space of worship where he could in the Spirit meet with the Friends towards whom God was directing him. I have experienced something of the sort myself, and I suspect it is commonly felt by travelling Friends.

Yet beyond this question, there is another thing which I want to recommend to your attention, which is: in reflecting on your devotional life as it relates to your concern for the gospel ministry, remember that a key part of our work in the ministry is understanding the nature of our gift—and I believe in consequence that our devotional life should reflect our real needs and gifts. To study widely or not, to keep a journal or not, to develop "rules of prayer" or not—these and many other technical questions are open, and to be answered by experimentation and experience. If in the quiet, one feels drawn to write, or to begin a systematic study of a book of the Bible, or the writings of a theologian, then try it conscientiously. If it feeds you, if you can keep it soaked in the sense of the Spirit's presence, if it feeds mind and heart, but not pride, then it may well be safe and nourishing. If it precludes a time of humble, expectant waiting, then it is taking too much space, because, as Penington says, the business of a Christian is to know Christ. In our reading and our reflection, in our waiting and in our writing, Christ's companionship and instruction should be present, even as we learn about history, or human psychology, or reflect on the needs of a friend. We are to seek the life of God in all.

Writing, whether in a journal or notebook or other form, can be a tremendous aid to reflection, and if you do not write reflectively in some form, I urge you to experiment with it. There are many "traps" to be avoided, any one of which, if you fall into it, could convince you that writing is not for you. While you can be guided by any of the genres of reflective writing that you've seen or heard about from others, treat these as avenues of exploration, rather than straitjackets whose "rules" you need to learn. The notes you take are for your own use. You don't need to write on a schedule, you don't need to use high-sounding language, you don't need to write finished prose, tell a continuous narrative of your life, or meet anyone else's expectations at all.

Your notes may be quotations from your reading, or telegraphic reminders of things you've heard people say. They may arise as part of your devotional reading, or your daily walks, or in relation to classes or workshops you attend. They may take the form of letters, or stories, or poems, or half-shaped phrases—or they may be a jumble of all of these.

I recommend three important characteristics for your journal or notebook: freedom, diversity, and cultivation.[7] By *freedom*, I mean that you write in the styles, and on the topics, that you find most useful at the time, and as honestly as possible. Your notebook, an extension and expression of your mind and spirit, should range as widely as you like and need to. Feel free to cut and paste from one document into another. The stuff you put in there is for your *use*. By *diversity*, I mean that you allow the material to be miscellaneous and to change over time: add in sketches or dried flowers or news clippings or anything that records your reflections usefully for your later use and information. Keep more than one kind of notebook for different kinds of material. Open new notebooks for specific projects, if that helps. Finally, *cultivation*: writing it down helps, but you need to read it, too. You are your own audience, and from time to time, you should extend the reflection that led to an entry by revisiting it, perhaps annotating it, adding to it or cross-referencing to other entries. In this way the notebook becomes a real tool for learning.

7 This framework is drawn from Drayton 2004.

If you find that your ministry includes writing for others (whether for publication or correspondence), this will shape the note-taking you do, of course, and the notes or journals may become places where ideas are explored more formally, in preparation for the creation of pieces for publication, or letters to be sent under concern.

I conclude this section with a wise quotation from Lewis Benson:

> The work of the prophetic minister is real work. It involves enriching his mind with the language of prophecy and the imagery of prophecy. It means finding time for the maturing of insights and the quiet prayer and meditation that leads to wisdom. It means meditating on the great themes of the Christian faith. These meditations will later enrich his ministry, but they are not rehearsals of sermons to be given at any particular time or place. (Benson 1979, 51)

8

Listening: inward prayer

For a minister, frequent listening is a fundamental part of the work, that is, it is the essential daily training for a life seeking to orient itself around a public service like the gospel ministry, which is so vulnerable to the needs of the self and the calculating mind. The development of some practice of prayer which fits your life is both an important achievement in itself, and the foundation for both growth and endurance. There are two modes which you should seek to realize. One is a dwelling in watchfulness—going through the day aware of God's presence, sometimes brought to the foreground by a brief shift of attention, often in the background. The other is a more purposeful time, in which we bring to the fore our intention to spend time with our friend and teacher. These of course may also be times for focused search on specific issues, and naturally the subjects will range across our whole lives. In the context of this book, however, I want to mention three tasks in which listening prayer seems especially important: evaluating your service, intercessory prayer, and listening in decisions.

Evaluating your service

You will probably often be tempted to over- or undervalue your service. When being conscious about a concern which includes so personal an outward performance as gospel ministry, one is easily drawn into this kind of instability. It is very hard not to evaluate one's actions for success or failure; it is also hard sometimes to see when something new should be attempted, or an old fear set down. It is, of course, needful to reflect upon one's doing or withholding; the difference in the fruitfulness of this reflection is in the light in which you reflect, the marks by which you judge, and the results you hope for. Therefore, listening in prayer is necessary as you learn how to see, test, taste, and value your ministry—the nature of the gift, and of your stewardship of it. You should seek to be able to pray honestly about your service, and expect to be shown what is missing, what is worth preserving, and what is to be rejected.

As ever, the first motion is to wait until you can feel the cool, quiet, strong flow of light and love. Wait until no content, no specific subject is before your mind. This most quiet stage may last briefly, but you must wait to reach it. Then allow the reflection to begin; but at many points, pause and feel for the springs of light again. Stay close to that quiet place, and then you will truly be able to regard your experience prayerfully.

Intercessory prayer

If you have not been in the habit of intercessory prayer, then you have not yet come to one of the necessary sources of instruction and discipline for service. This is a kind of prayer that comes easily to some, but is more difficult for others; it may be because intercessory prayer, "praying for someone," raises central questions about the nature of prayer. My own experience with intercessory prayer has included long periods of not-knowing—and in those times, I have not practiced prayer at all. I believe that in waiting, and longing for guidance, I was led into a place of renewal in prayer. The result has been that, though I may not be great in prayer, I am at home with it, in its sweet manifestations and its bitter. In case it is of use, I would like to set down here something of what I do.

When I first was experimenting with intercession, all I could feel to do was to articulate some desire or request on someone's behalf. At times this could seem alive and real. At other times, I found myself straining or worrying, trying to figure out what to pray for, and falling back into vague and quite formulaic good wishes for the objects of my prayer. I am sure that the Lord accepted these for whatever good intent was in them, but it did not feel like a productive path.

I discovered quite another way during an unexpected opportunity with a beloved older minister; it has been my usual pattern ever since. At first we were sitting, each at a desk on opposite sides of the room, quite unconnected, each occupied with some work of his own. Quite suddenly I felt that my friend had dropped into prayer, and even though our backs were to each other (because of how the furniture was arranged in the room we were using), I was drawn into a real place of quiet reverence. It was in that quiet, unforced sense of the beloved presence of God, shared with my friend, that I felt myself praying in quite a different way, first for others, and then at last for myself, something I had never been free to do before. The memory of that time remains fresh and sweet to me.

The lesson I learned then was, it is good to spend some time in a wordless, unstriving sense of the presence of God, in which my only purposeful act is to direct my attention towards someone I wish to pray for. Sitting in the light, I see the person in that light, and in a sense I just stand together with him or her in the presence.

In that time, I am just aware of my cherishing that person, and his or her deepest welfare, as though I am telling God that I care for him or her, and asking God to do so, too. Sometimes I am led into a reverent and searching reflection on something about that person's life or condition. I may even be able to feel a place where they may be challenged or the life oppressed in them.

From this meditation may arise some sense that I should speak or write to them, or do something for them. Sometimes, though, I am left only with a sense of fresh awareness about these individuals (or subjects), or a clearer knowledge of them. This sense of intensified awareness is a fruit worthy of much gratitude for its own sake, and a major contributor to serviceability in word, deed, or silent ministry. After a time, the image is released, and I can leave the place of prayer, or move on to some other focus.

I have also found that it is good to spend some time just waiting openly in the presence to allow a face, or group, or concern, to rise up unsought for. When this happens, I feel particularly attentive to who or what arises, and to any particular motions relative to the subject. Very often, the result is nothing more than an education for me—I become more aware of the name, face, group, or issue that arises, and therefore, I am just a little better prepared to listen, pray, learn, or act in the future. Sometimes, the subject that arises may take on a more focused importance, and then it may be that a concern or leading is taking shape.

Listening in decisions

Listening in the midst of deciding is an exercise that all Friends should be practicing in our lives, but perhaps we do not indulge in it as much as we could. For a minister, this is something that should grow to be very usual practice, more especially if we are deciding about any religious service—and we should bear in mind how hard we find it to do, and how many lessons we may have to learn in attempting to be faithful in it.

While it may be that Friends very generally seek divine guidance in their daily lives, we tend not to speak of it, and that is regrettable, as some more open testimony in this connection might be helpful to others. To that end, I briefly note here my own practice. I can mention three kinds of listening that I have learned to do when deciding.

First, a quick inward retirement—a momentary pause, a brief period of mindfulness, in which God and the decision are both in my awareness. If no prohibition arises, then I feel free to proceed as seems best upon other considerations. I imagine that this is the commonest way Friends "check in" during the day, and it was discovered early among us. Hugh Barbour writes of it as part of the daily practice of Quakers even in the early period: "In some ordinary activities, no special guidance was looked for, and it was enough that Friends found within themselves no contrary balks or 'stops to their minds.'" (Barbour 1964, 114) This is the kind of listening that I try to do at work and around the house, and it can be a powerful if very simple tool for noticing places where I have allowed myself to become encumbered to the impairment of my spiritual health.

Second, "sanctified debate." By this phrase I mean simply taking time to become deeply aware of the presence, and then undertaking an intentional meditation and reflection on the decision. This allows my reasons pro and con to be examined in the consciousness of my deepest commitment, and thus to allow the light to a certain degree to search my motives, fears, and hopes. I may find then that I refrain from something, because I see that to act on it on the basis of my most prominent motives would be a betrayal, large or small, of my sense of the divine truth that I have; or would serve to harden me against something that is uncomfortable but important—something that is making me less tender (and here I might include even just too much busyness).

Finally, "seeking the opening way." I have sometimes found that when I sit with a decision, there is no prohibition or stop that directs my choice (by eliminating an alternative). Nor do my reasonings produce clarity. If I feel I must act, then I have found it good to wait until I feel a path opening as I look in one direction or another, and a sense of release or freedom when I contemplate taking that route. Then, even if I feel doubts or concerns, unless these intensify, I go ahead in trust.

Recently, a Friend told me of another practice that seems very similar. He told me that when faced with a choice of which city to go to for a medical procedure, he waited, and felt that City A had "more light on it" than City B, so he went to A and felt that all went well. Not long after hearing that story, I found that John Churchman, in his journal, speaks of this practice as well. Since hearing from my friend, I have in decision making paid attention to this sense of light, and found it is a good additional technique for living more mindfully.

I wish to emphasize that I do not recount these practices of mine as in any way representing a manual of prayer, nor as if they are of any profundity. I write of it only because it is part of the work of a minister to grow in listening prayer, in more and more settings, and I have been encouraged and instructed to hear others' practice and experience in this regard. Over the years, these considerations have become part of my learning to keep the daily watch, as faithfully as I can.

9
Listening: scripture

People have different *feelings* about scripture, beyond any ideas about it they may have. For some people, it feels like a mountain they have to climb, or a duty which they really ought to honor, though they don't feel pleasure in the prospect. For some, it is an authority, either to rely upon, or to rebel against, or to use in some company but not others. Some people enjoy it as an encounter, almost like travel in a distant country partially known—some places familiar, always some surprises, but a trip undertaken with confidence and real relish. Some people just ignore it. The list of feelings about scripture is quite long, and of course each of us may feel any or many of these at different times in our lives, and sometimes simultaneously. Nevertheless, find a way to read scripture frequently and deeply—and actively. If it is not part of your practice, I urge you to make it so. If this is not easy for you, I suggest that the most important thing is to stay engaged with scripture, become familiar with its many moods and dimensions, and take what meaning you can from it each time.

It is often a first impulse in these days to tackle the scriptures intellectually, acknowledging the great distances of time and culture that make them often inscrutable. The Advices encourage us to study them regularly, making use of modern aids to understanding and interpretation. This intellectual approach is a "cool," careful way to start to know the scriptures, if you are not comfortable reading them. Furthermore, such study, if it deepens our familiarity with the text, can be enriching and invaluable.

However, I would recommend in addition to any such study you may undertake, that you make sure to spend time just reading them when you are centered and aware of the divine presence. Start reading slowly, not trying to interpret or translate, but just with the feelings and imagination, and an inwardly open attitude. When something rises up, catches your attention, read it over several times slowly, and then stop reading and let it echo in your mind. You may form definite ideas about it, you may even write them down, but the most important thing is to read them in the spirit, receiving them as you do someone's ministry that comes quietly amidst a gathered meeting. George Fox spoke of reading the scriptures in the same spirit in which they were given forth, and if we dwell deeply, when reading, we can feel somewhat how it may have felt to hear or even write the words; in any case they are as if new.

Now, there are many good reasons to become conversant with scripture, and all of them enrich our spirits and our service. The point which I wish to emphasize for present purposes, however, is this one: We are as liable as any people in history to fall prey to idolatry, and a habit of honest encounter with scripture is one way to combat this tendency.

By "idolatry," of course, I do not mean the obvious, old-fashioned paganism, offering worship to images of God or gods, but giving in to our tendency to mistake the human for the divine, the façade for the substance, and in short, to worship gods of our own making, who bear an eerie resemblance to ourselves. We thus are all too prone to shape a religion for ourselves that is unchallenging and comfy, and we bow down to an image in a mirror. This may be particularly easy in Quakerism, which nowadays does not even enforce eccentric clothing or unusual speech upon us. How easy it is to feel we are simple, peaceable, Spirit-led, faithful, when we may in truth be merely conventionally moral, fearful, and shy of conflict! In the struggle to get past our comforting illusions, and reach towards a God of truth, whose love is also judgment, and whose light both convicts and heals us to be stronger than we were before, a habit of grappling with the scriptures at all the levels of feelings, imagination, intellect, and prayer is a powerful help indeed. As our inward life takes on new dimensions of experience and truthfulness, our encounter with scripture will become more vivid and important for us.

10

Listening: Friends tradition

What gain is there in listening to the voice of tradition, especially in a religious movement in which "continuing revelation" is a deeply-held value? For me, the fundamental reason to listen carefully to Quaker tradition is the oneness of God, and the human tendency to take our own customs, ideas, values, and commitments as revelation. I believe that Quakerism truly arose under a fresh in-coming of the spirit of Christ, and under its guidance the first Quakers in a remarkably short time were led into a way of walking as Friends of the truth, and Children of the light (of Christ), a way with its own integrity.

It is true that God, whatever God is, has been in operation among all peoples in all times, yet this does not mean that all aspects of all cultures are manifestations of (His, Her, Its) action and guidance, any more than all of our culture is consonant with God's will and spirit. How shall we separate the godly from the ungodly elements in our living? While nineteenth century liberal theologians liked to talk about humans' progress in their understanding of God, and today's process theologians can speak of processes and change within God as well as in human understandings of God, I find a different metaphor more useful, one that I suppose borrows more from science than anything else.

One might say that since the early stages of Judaism, through to the times of Jesus, and then through the ages of Christianity to the rise of Quakerism, a certain theory about the relation of God and humanity has been slowly under development.[8] As with any powerful and comprehensive theoretical structure (for example, evolutionary biology), some areas will be well developed and move beyond question, while

---

[8] This view, a theory of successive choices of interpretation, explicitly rejects the theory about the relation of Judaism to Christianity known as supercessionism.

others are more debatable. The general thrust of the theory remains coherent, however, if it has any explanatory power at all, even as bits are pruned, added, or deeply refurbished. It is by recognizing and working with the consistent architecture that progress is made at the frontiers of ignorance.

Quakerism represents a relatively recent theory about Christianity, and while we must be humble about the vast possibilities for confusing human preferences and culture with revelation about the nature and actions of the divine, yet Quakerism as a structure by the early 1700s had developed into a consistent and powerful "theory." That is, it had developed on the basis of the great openings of the 1650s into a web of practice, faith, and experience, in which all parts are interdependent. It provided a coherent fabric of life, whose primary purpose and design was to enable us to live under the immediate guidance of the spirit of Christ, in our worship, our church affairs, and our daily activities as well, with far-reaching implications for civic affairs, social justice, and all other aspects of human life.

Now, was this fabric complete? Was it perfectly faithful to, reflective of, divine guidance? Must it be normative for our time in all respects? Of course not. Yet one of the things about the modernist era in which we live is the cultural conviction that the most recent is the most authentic, the thing we know best and feel most comfortable with is to be taken most seriously. Such assumptions are productive to a certain degree, but they must always be put to the test; and at their worst, or at our most heedless, they can encourage self-indulgence and the sort of idolatry that reshapes the world and the God we worship after our own image.

Yet God moves now, and has moved in the past. Traces of the Quaker experience of divine activity is embodied in Quaker tradition in various forms—in documents and journals from the past, stories and folklore, as well as in the discipline, testimonies, language, and customs that are still distinctive to us. These are all the results of lives lived in the Quaker way, under the guidance of the Spirit. To repeat a passage of Penington's:

"the Lord hath appeared in others, as well as to me; yea, there are others who are in the growth of his truth, and in the purity and dominion of his life, far beyond me." (Penington 1995–7, 2:372)

Therefore, on this basis alone, it is valuable for a modern Friend to become deeply familiar with the Quaker tradition in its various forms, and to understand it in relationship to its original purpose, as a way to live faithfully in the Spirit, rather than a set of customs now outgrown, or a set of beliefs.

But I have been writing in intellectual or theological tones, and this is only the surface of the matter. In this seeking, as in all your inward research, the goal is to feel after the life. Just as you should seek to be aware, habitually, of the light in the people you meet, and seek for the spiritual in the events of your time and your own experiences, it is important to find out why a particular aspect of Quaker practice arose, in relation to the fundamental drive to contain Spirit in temporal life, and remember that many aspects of the Quaker "system" were mutually reinforcing, and therefore plucking one to eliminate or emphasize, by itself in isolation from the whole system, may ignore or distort its actual, systematic meaning.[9]

As I have lived with the concern for the ministry for many years, I have often been drawn into places of sympathy and understanding with regard to ministers of earlier times, others who carried the concern I now feel. On the basis of the common work, and some similar experience, I have found myself able sometimes to see from their point of view, and to understand something of the freshness and clarity with which they regarded aspects of Quaker practice and spirituality that before I had not felt any real connection to. In this way, as I felt my way a little into their condition, I was better able to learn from them. Often this sympathy has enabled me to recognize when their writings, often so opaque at first, were speaking of tangible, spiritual conditions and events that I could connect with, and be challenged as well as instructed by.

[9] In appendix 1 I discuss the question of the recording of ministers from this point of view.

I am not a "plain Friend," nor am I anything but a person of my times. My religious experience reflects my own life history, talents, social milieu, and limitations, as anyone's does. I am not advising a return to the past. On the contrary, from my own experience and practice I can report remarkable sources of inner nourishment—spiritual, emotional, and intellectual—when I have borne in mind that God has spoken to others as well as to me, and when I have taken seriously the bond that the Spirit makes within our community, both with contemporaries and with Friends of the past. Though this effort brings conflict with it, as well as other blessings that are easier to accept and understand, it is a vital consequence of our faith in God as a reliable teacher.

We are not alone, we few thousand modern Friends, and our community has not arisen just in our life-times as Friends. The living tree is growing and active in its leaves, and the thin, outer layers of cells that surround the wood laid down in years past. But this year's life would not be possible without the tissues laid down last year, and in all the decades before.

11

Motions of love and the parable of the sower: the content of ministry

I determined not to know anything among you except Jesus Christ, and him crucified. (1 Cor 2:2)

We are to feel where the seed, the divine life, dwells in those we are drawn to serve; to feel how it is oppressed in them, as in ourselves; to sympathize with them as they seek to pass through the experience prefigured by Jesus' crucifixion and triumph, into fuller, freer life.

Samuel Bownas and later writers on the ministry (for example Joseph John Dymond, John Graham, and John W. Rowntree) have written at some length about the content of ministry. The typical content of ministry in meetings has changed with time; it is instructive to compare the ministry you have heard with the many sermons available at the Quaker homiletics home page.[10] Sermons there include lengthy doctrinal arguments, extended Biblical expositions, searching and detailed addresses on personal conduct, forceful denunciations of unrighteousness in private and public life. In addition, either as separate pieces or as part of larger discourses, there are relatively brief messages, often only a few sentences, exhorting the listeners to turn to the light, mind the inward monitor, live faithful to the light given. Some of these brief messages offer consolation in troubles and grief, and are very tender in their tone.

From a reading of memorials to deceased ministers, as in the nineteenth century series *The Annual Monitor,* or collections published by various yearly meetings, I think it likely that most messages in most meetings were relatively brief, exhortatory, and saturated with Biblical quotation. As Howard Brinton writes, an important aim of the ministry in such messages was to encourage Friends to enter a certain emotional/spiritual space, creating awe and accessibility to the Spirit:

[10] www.qhpress.org/quakerpages/qhoa/qhoa.htm

> The preaching [in my boyhood meeting] was of the oracular, prophetic type . . . always a simple, direct appeal for obedience to the inward admonitions of the Spirit. Its object was to arouse religious feelings rather than religious ideas. . . . Although as small boys we invented games to pass the time in meeting, sometimes even we felt the wind of the Spirit blow over us, as from a supernatural world beyond and above. Our response was awe, wonder, and reverence. . . . The Wilburite type of sermon, though not concerned with a logical presentation of ideas, often had in it a quickening, elevating, purging effect which no intellectual discourse about doctrines or social concerns, however edifying, can convey. (Brinton 1960, 6)

I know of no systematic study that has been done on recent Quaker sermons, but I suspect that such a study is likely to demonstrate that modern Quaker messages show a strong tendency to brevity, and messages that tend to be either personal reflection and testimony, or statements on social issues. A topical consideration, however, is perhaps not the most valuable for our present purposes; so I would like to consider the "Parable of the Sower":

> A sower went out to sow his seed; and as he sowed, some fell by the way side; and it was trodden down, and the fowls of the air devoured it. And some fell upon a rock; and as soon as it was sprung up, it withered away, because it lacked moisture. And some fell among thorns; and the thorns sprang up with it, and choked it. And other fell on good ground, and sprang up, and bare fruit a hundredfold. (Luke 8:5–8)

The aim and concern of the ministry is to help the life of God to take root and flourish in the hearts and lives of men and women, bearing fruit in good works and a life lived in the clarity of the light. It is for this reason that the differing fates of the seed are good to think on. There are so many ways in which we can allow the word received in the heart to be snatched away, or choked out, or suppressed by the press of challenges to our strength and patience. Whether it forms the content of messages or not, the minister should spend much time meditating not only on ideas, and scripture, and events, but also on the human condition. This includes the ways we are tempted, the ways we presume to run before we walk, the ways we mistake our own needs and inclinations for something divine, the ways we fail in love, and rush into judgment and partisanship, the ways we do not rule our tongues, or improve our talents, the ways we cede our autonomy to our society, or peers, or job, or habits, or appetites. We should become aware of the mind-forged manacles which we all tend to wear, unless the spirit frees us, and we follow promptly and humbly, testing our new hope with faithfulness and persistence.

It is important to remember in our meditations that while culture changes, and history marches on, and 2005 is different from 1492, and so on, yet humans are the same creatures, with the same dilemmas. Each new child born into the world must discover how to live in love, to reckon with fear, to accept death, to maintain hope. No matter how much technology there is, or how much of a social network surrounds us, we still all start at the beginning, meet grief and exaltation and desire and despair, do good and evil and have to live with the consequences. None of us should in our spiritual lives forget this primal, basic, simple truth about ourselves and those around us, the basic news about motives, needs, hopes, and illusions. The minister most of all must meditate, like Jesus, on what is in the human heart (Jn 2:25), and work out of a desire for everyone's enjoyment of God's presence and fellowship.

> From an inward purifying and steadfast abiding under it, springs a lively operative desire for the good of others. All faithful people are not called to the public ministry, but whoever are, are called to minister of that which they have tasted and handled spiritually. The outward modes of worship are various, but wherever men are true ministers of Jesus Christ, it is from the operation of his spirit upon their hearts, first purifying them, and thus giving them a feeling sense of the conditions of others. (Woolman 1971, 31)

Whatever our gifts and style of ministry, we must come to see how to observe, reflect, and experience our lives, and feel where our commonalities are with our brothers and sisters. We must gain practice in bringing every change of weather, every chance and sorrow and triumph before God in stillness and confidence, and allow the light to play over and through it. Through this inward research we come to understand in compassion and honesty the journey towards "salvation," which is freedom in the spirit from bondage.

> Dear Hearts, you make your own troubles, by being unwilling and disobedient to that which would lead you. I see there is no way but to go hand in hand with him in all things, running after him without fear or considering, leaving the whole work only to him. If he seem to smile, follow him in fear and love; and if he seem to frown, follow him, and fall into his will, and you shall see he is yours still. (Nayler, Letter to George Fox and others, Drayton 1994, 77)

It is for this reason that the fundamental message, which we may more and more feel to be present under or around or behind the present message, is that of the divine love and light at work and available, with which we can reconcile and cooperate. Yet that light and life is oppressed and hindered in its growth in us: the Christ life is crucified and suffering. Gospel ministry has its root and purpose in the experience of the seed's presence, growth and health, and of its oppression under many burdens—encouraging the life where it springs up, and identifying and combating the oppression. "I was determined to know nothing among you but Christ and him crucified."

The preaching of early Friends had power not because of its sociology, not because of its politics, but because they knew themselves as part of the drama of salvation, their story was the latest chapter in the story that began with Adam and moved through Noah, Moses, the prophets, Jesus and the apostles. They were seeing in their own time the dawning of the gospel day, and the fresh action of God inviting them to freedom from the bondage of sin, and the overcoming of darkness with light. Sometimes the story was told so as to embrace the great movements of history, sometimes it was made as simple and particular as admonitions to honesty in business, avoidance of war taxes, living gently on the earth. In each of these themes, large or small, cosmic or intimate, the great story is seen unfolding.

> Over and over again, through an infinite variety of messages, each of which they believed was specifically given by the Spirit for that specific occasion, [the ministers] called people out of the darkness surrounding ordinary human nature, into the light which can transform that human nature through spiritual communion with the living Christ . . . the initial entrance into the light [w]as only a preliminary, though necessary, step; the real question was whether a person would continue, throughout life, to move along with the light. To deny the light at any point might mean that it would be lost. Thus, the infinite variety of Quaker sermons was frequently aimed, like a surgeon's scalpel, at deftly exposing that little sin or that great omission which a specific Friend was allowing to cloud his access to the light. (Taber 1980, 12–13)

Finally, out of that growing inner experience, you will find yourself treasuring the work that has brought you along, and finding joy in it. More than that, you will be happy to feel where a desire for service is rising in anyone, and to encourage it. You will come to feel how important it is to encourage others to consider the ministry as a primary concern, but you will also be more and more aware of the power of God moving in any kind of concern, and feel the kinship among all kinds of service that are rooted in love and compassion. You will be glad to see this work going on, and grateful enough to thank others for their faithfulness. This may often be the most important act a minister can perform, to encourage someone else as they try to do their part.

Joseph Hoag wrote of how, while he was wrestling with the sense that he was being called into the ministry, David Sands paid him a visit in his home to do this very thing:

> Almost as soon as he entered the door, he singled me out, and not only told me that the call was right, but took hold of the reasonings and difficulties I had passed through for years, more

correctly than I could myself. Then, in this moving language, said, "As sure as thou knowest all this to be true, so sure thy exercise, thy concern, and thy call is right; and if thou wilt give up and be faithful, the Lord will be thy strength, and thy reward, and will surely carry thee through all thy straits . . . thou hast many trials to pass through, but the Lord will be thy leader and thy rearward." (Hoag 1861, 44)

12

Varieties of service: no mold

It can't be said strongly enough: there is no one right way to serve in the gospel ministry, aside from faithfulness to God's direction. As Richard Bauman once wrote, a Quaker minister has to do both *everything* and *nothing*, that is, everything he or she is led to do by the Spirit, and nothing that he or she is not led to do. (Bauman 1983)

Therefore, in learning the shape of your particular gift, or in considering that of others, let yourself be informed and stimulated but not enthralled by others' examples, as one source of instruction in your schooling as a skilled and committed servant. As I sit in reflection on this subject, several people come to mind whom I have known and whose ministry is precious to me. (I keep the pictures anonymous, and in the past tense, though most of these people are living still.)

- She came to meeting every week, a dignified older woman neatly turned out, sitting in the same spot on the same bench. Once or twice a month, she would rise to speak early in the meeting. Her messages typically included personal reflections, scripture quotation, and stories from her childhood, in what at first seemed a stream of consciousness, a garrulous, good-hearted flow. Yet listening week after week, one came to see how important she felt it was for the children in meeting to hear ministry that they could connect with, yet not be talked down to; and it was clear that she had a store of memories, scripture reading, and literature upon which she often reflected, and drew from freely and naturally in ministry. She was not seen often as a leader in the meeting, did not travel to other meetings under concern, but over the years left a powerful and very sweet impression on many of her Friends.

- An older man, who almost never spoke in meeting, was chiefly loved for his gift of sympathetic listening and quiet, wise conversation. Genial and soft-spoken, his quiet manner accompanied a passionate character. He took the practice of daily retirement and reflection very seriously, and steadfastly meditated on his reading in scripture, biography, church history, devotional literature, and public affairs. He was extraordinarily gifted in encouragement and at listening. Often you would find that, weeks after a conversation, he had been mulling over some statement he'd heard, and felt drawn to take up the topic again, enriched by his prayer and thought. He was especially effective at encouraging younger people who spoke in meeting, his quiet comments showing that he had been listening with interest, reverence, and good judgment both to what was said, and what might lie behind the words—hidden even from the speaker.

- Another Friend comes to mind, cheerful and direct, deeply steeped in scripture from her youth, and gifted in prayer and song. Her tireless travels among Friends in Africa and the western hemisphere gave her an amazing acquaintance with Quakerdom of all kinds, and especially at the level of meetings and individuals. Her particular concern was to encourage those not often encouraged— women, youth leaders, other ministers. Her ministry in meeting was often brief and simple, and usually ended in a short prayer; but her concern was enacted in many other channels, by correspondence, conversation, and fellowship. She was often a spreader of news and ideas from meeting to meeting, sometimes merely by scooping up newsletters from here, and taking them there, sometimes by connecting people or meetings who should know about each other. Any time together, with a single person, a committee, or a meeting, was a chance to recognize a blessing.

- My final example is a Friend who offered occasional ministry in meeting. His deepening study of Friends' belief, and of the scriptures, led him to start offering workshops on topics he was exploring. As he gained experience, and continued deepening his devotional life, and his engagement with his meeting, his ministry both in meetings and in workshops became deeper, sweeter, and in some ways more daring, because more open and searching. During this time, he came to see that he had a clear leading to a teaching ministry, and other ways perhaps opening as well.

These Friends do not fit the pattern of the modern public Friend, of which I have given no thumbnail as such Friends are widely known, and to be seen, for example, at most yearly meeting sessions. Their portrait must be added to this little gallery, of course—the Friends of stature who are called upon for specific events, whether to lead workshops or give talks or presentations. If these opportunities are undertaken after discernment, and with a real concern to act as guided by God, such opportunities can move beyond conventional form, and be the occasion for gospel ministry. Arrangements for ministers to attend specific places at specific times date from the beginning of the Society. J. S. Rowntree wrote about the way that the Second Day Morning Meeting would plan to ensure that meetings in the London area, especially small or out-of-the-way meetings, were visited by known ministering Friends:

> It is sometimes implied, if not said, that it exhibits some lack of spirituality for a Friend to allow his [sic] name to be put down on a plan to attend a certain meeting at an appointed hour. Evidently this was not felt by George Whitehead, William Penn, Ambrose Rigg, and Samuel Bownas. . . . Probably in nine cases out of ten, a minister has no special drawing to one meeting above another—he has a freedom to go where his friends think him the most wanted. In the case of his having a "concern" for one meeting, way would be made for his giving effect to such an apprehension of duty. (Doncaster 1908, 271)

Of course, such an arrangement then leaves open the question, how the invited Friend will work to enable her service to be guided by the Spirit under the conditions of the arrangement, and different Friends have reached different conclusions about this matter.

The point is that Friends in the gospel ministry have had very different kinds of service, and it is good to review some of the varieties, if only to help the reader in considering his or her own gift, or that of others.

First a note about travel, which is treated more extensively in chapter 24. Friends may be called to exercise their gifts either in their home meeting, or at other meetings. It is not often recognized how much variety in practice there was, even during the "golden age" of travelling ministers, in the eighteenth and nineteenth centuries. There are extensive records of the activities of Friends ministers during this period—journals, memorial minutes, and publications such as the *Annual Monitor*, which came out for many years with short obituaries of Friends who had died recently, very many of them ministers. A survey of these indicates that service by ministers was first and foremost in and around the home monthly meeting[11] and neighboring meetings, then somewhat less often more widely within the yearly meeting; and least often beyond the bounds of the yearly meeting. For example, in one count of about 50 such records, I found that 95 percent of the records indicated service in or near the monthly meeting; 66 percent mentioned visitation within the yearly meeting; and 39 percent mentioned travel beyond the yearly meeting. In a significant number of cases, the visits to other yearly meetings were only within the bounds of the nearest yearly meeting (for example, travel from New England to New York, or from Great Britain to Ireland).

Even a great traveller like Elias Hicks did most of his travel within the bounds of his yearly meeting.[12] Out of approximately 60 minutes for service which he received from his meeting, five were specifically for family visits in meetings on Long Island; 29 for travel to meetings within New York Yearly Meeting; five for

[11] Recall that during the eighteenth and nineteenth centuries, it was common for one monthly meeting to include several worshipping congregations.

[12] For this reckoning I rely on the listing of minutes given as an appendix in Forbush 1956.

special concerns within the yearly meeting (e.g. to schools on Long Island, to Long Island Indians, to new meetings within the yearly meeting). About ten minutes were granted for more extensive travel, to three or more yearly meetings, and almost all of these were for service lasting fewer than six months.

Thus, while it is true that the travelling ministers were an important part of the circulation of life within the Religious Society of Friends (for the most part preserving a shared culture, though also exacerbating the separations), and while it is also true that there were at any one time many ministers travelling across the Atlantic, and amongst the United States and the maritime provinces of Canada—still, the highest volume of circulation was within the bounds of yearly meetings.

Now, about modalities. By this I mean, what kinds of things have Friends done, either when travelling or at home? Again, there has always been a wide range of concerns, and gifts for them, and degrees of skill or effectiveness in each.

Preaching in meeting on First Days is one gift that actually has historically included several types, often noted in journals or other accounts. For example, some Friends particularly excel at vocal prayer, others at the use of scriptural material to illuminate some topic. Some say only a few words at a time, and some speak at more length. Some have had much psychological insight, and been gifted at exposing people's misconceptions, breaking down their sense of self-sufficiency, and opening people to the light (a "plowing" or "planting" ministry). Some are especially gifted at reaching to those who are young in their spiritual lives, and need encouragement and help in developing and deepening their practice (a "watering ministry"). Some have focused on ethics and social concerns, some on theological or doctrinal topics. There are well-known cases of Friends who have a particular calling to reach out to non-Friends, and rarely speak in their home meeting at all. I can think of one Friend with great gifts of preaching, counsel, and "presence" whose primary calling seems to be to a Latin American yearly meeting, where her gifts are called on intensively, and welcomed gratefully.

Others find that their concern is worked out best in other settings such as in writing, in teaching forums and workshops, in opportunities (see chapters 20 and 21 below), or in family visits of a more systematic nature. J.B. Braithwaite's children wrote of their father:

> As a minister of the gospel, he saw openings that had never before presented themselves, and the work needing to be done was more than he could cope with . . . much of his early ministerial work was done among his own people, either in Westmoreland or in London and Middlesex. . . . This work near home was carried on during the ordinary course of life. Legal work during the week, often with pastoral visits in the evenings; First Day spent at some outlying meeting, with all the spaces between meeting diligently made use of—such is very commonly the arduous life of an earnest Quaker minister. (Thomas 1919, 132)

Understanding the shape of your concern at the present time is part of keeping close to the gift. However, it is also worth asking yourself, is more called for? Have I not seen an opening for service, merely because I did not imagine it to be possible? It seems to me very likely that we do not have all the ministry we need, in all the varied forms that would really cultivate and nourish the life in our meetings, and that many gifts of service and witness remain underused and poorly developed, because there are not enough Friends with the experience, commitment, tact, and imagination to notice, pray for, encourage, and give thanks for their Friends' gifts and talents. After all, while you or I may have some gift or leading, it is of no effect if it is not received, and as noted above, one of the most important functions of a minister is to be eager to find others getting engaged in their own proper service. Therefore, I recommend to you, reader, that you inquire, alone and with a confidante, whether there are not other kinds of service that you might render. Remember the old story of the elder who comes to a young Friend and asks him if he might possibly have a calling to the ministry. The younger Friend replies "I have not had that concern." The older Friend shoots back "But has thee had the concern to have the concern?" "Covet earnestly the best gifts," and "work while it is day!"

Another quotation from Penn's *Rise and Progress* emphasizes alertness for opportunities to serve:

> I beseech you that you would not think it sufficient to declare the Word of life in their assemblies, however edifying and comfortable such opportunities may be to you and them; but . . . to inquire into the state of the several churches you visit; who among them are afflicted or sick, who are tempted, and if any are unfaithful or obstinate; and endeavor to issue those things in the wisdom and power of God . . . the afflicted will be comforted by you, the tempted strengthened, the sick refreshed, the unfaithful convicted and restored, and such as are obstinate, softened and fitted for reconciliation. (Penn 1980, 72)

13

On the ordering of the Holy Spirit

The Advice, "Bring the whole of your life under the ordering of the Holy Spirit" is a central challenge for anyone under concern, and it may especially be so for you if you are faithful and useful in the ministry. This is because the exercise of the gift is a kind of leadership, and makes one visible—hence the ancient label of "public Friend." As Edward Hicks once wrote, "my public character is certainly a kind of public property." (Hicks 1851, 128) Your experiments and experience with this spiritual work, the heart of simplicity, are important for several reasons. First, it is our calling as followers of Jesus; second, this ordering and clarifying of your life is likely to be necessary if you are to be faithful to your calling to service in the ministry; and finally, it will provide you insight and understanding about how hard it is, and how a dependence upon God's guidance and power are at the heart of our success in this endeavor. All of this should season your ministry and deepen your charity towards others struggling with the same choices.

Most Friends are aware of the challenges of balancing our work lives and our spiritual lives—but even as I write that, I hope that you who are reading it are thinking, Isn't our goal to "bring the *whole* of life" under the ordering of the Spirit? Furthermore, the work of getting a livelihood is an important source of instruction and insight on many levels, from the personal to the social and political. If we are careful, our jobs are ways to serve and also to witness with our lives. Yet there are times when one kind of work is in the foreground, and the other seems to recede. It is a mark of maturity that we are increasingly aware that God is nearby, in a benevolent and sanctifying sense, throughout the day. The balance is always dynamic, however, because all our actions draw on our limited stock of time. The challenge for a Friend under concern is to work with that dynamic balance consciously.

The work of spiritual nurture requires some time of focus, in devotional reading, silent reflection and prayer, and the other exercises we may be led to. Giving one's economic and social demands their due—but no more than their due—is never easy, and for most ministers there is not one final solution, but a frequent consideration and attention to the question over the course of one's life. Bill Taber conjectured on the basis of his study and experience that probably the majority of Friends ministers were not rich. Sometimes an acceptance of one's calling means also accepting that success in business life will be limited, because even if you throw yourself conscientiously and even with joy into your job, you must reserve some of your time and energy—and not the dregs—for your service in ministry. I have found it so.

John Woolman's description of a time when he made an adjustment in his business life, so it would take no more than its share of his time and attention is well known, but worth considering again:

> The increase of business became my burden, for though my natural inclination was toward merchandise, yet I believed Truth required me to live more free from outward cumbers, and in this exercise my prayers were put up to the Lord, who graciously heard me and gave me a heart inclined to his holy will. Then I lessened my outward business, and as I had opportunity told my customers of my intentions, that they might consider what shop to turn to, and so in a while wholly laid down merchandise, following my trade as a tailor, myself only, having no apprentice. I also had a nursery of apple trees, in which I employed some of my time—hoeing, grafting, trimming, and inoculating. (Woolman 1971, 53–54)

It is well to remember, however, that it is not only one's livelihood that can create "outward cumber." Job Scott wrote about this particular kind of cumber, arising from over activity in Quaker affairs:

> I have found it my business, sometimes of late, to be more inward in travail, and less active in the exercise of the wholesome rules of society [i.e. the Religious Society of Friends] than

I once was; and believe, when I have obeyed the call into this inward, still abode, and there felt my loins rightly girded, it has contributed much more to the right exercise of the discipline, than when, through a desire for its proper administration, I have, by overacting, seemed to do a good deal for its execution. (Scott *Journal* 1831, 1:133)

"Meeting work" can take up rather more time than is appropriate, and I find myself every year, during "nominating season," asking myself what might be my limits and freedom in this connection. On the one hand, I want to be of use, and to take my fair share; on the other hand, if I am really concerned to work in the ministry, that is, in fact, an important portion of my share. I need to make sure that on the one hand I do not shirk it, and on the other hand I contribute in other ways as I feel free to, when my Friends request.

To offer a concrete example of one Friend's "balancing act," I here note my own practice. For the past few years, I have tried to limit workshop or similar commitments to three per year (an arbitrary number), and turned down most committee assignments. However, I have made this part of my discipline explicit to my meeting, to give them an opportunity to advise me if they think I need to make a change. In my report to my meeting for 2004, I wrote:

My job is demanding, and this coming year will perhaps be more so, so I need to be sure that my Quaker work takes an appropriate amount of my time, and no more. If I look back over 2005, and have done fewer things, but done them well, I will be satisfied. I should also say that I am not easy in my mind about my service within our meeting. That is, I am not sure that I have been seeking hard enough to perceive openings in which I might contribute more. I will continue as [monthly meeting] clerk through the coming year, but I am not clear that I should continue beyond that. It may well be time (or more than time!) for someone else to take that role. I am also open to any guidance or suggestions from the meeting about other ways that I might help, which I have not seen for myself.

14
On growth in the gift: learning from the work

You will find it profitable to examine, from time to time, what happens when you exercise your gift. Much material for reflection arises when you act, as you believe, upon a call to service. Some of this material comes as feedback of various kinds. For example, people may receive the service as you expected, but they may not. The response may be unexpectedly negative or positive. From the nature of content of the response, you get some information about the condition of those you thought to serve, as well as your own discernment about when to speak or keep silent, and what to say.

A second kind of feedback comes from analysis in hindsight, which may have its roots in promptings from the Spirit, to show you your condition. When you sit down after speaking, or next find a quiet moment of openness, you may feel an inward rebuke, a sense stealing over you, perhaps, that you were wrong, or ill-timed, or that you acted from a mistaken motive. Even if objectively it felt "good," or Friends express satisfaction, you may still hear inwardly "I have not required this at your hand."

> If the call is really from God strength will be given. If not, the minister will feel a gentle rebuke and inner disquiet after he has spoken. Experience will teach him to distinguish between a sense of uncertainty that comes from God and human uncertainty. (Benson 1979, 49)

Worse, you may realize or suspect that you undertook the work quite cold-bloodedly, because you felt it was expected of you, or because you were anxious that someone should do something, or had reason to believe such a message would "do the meeting good." The work may have been prompted because your own estimate of yourself required it.

A third kind of feedback is to be found in your personal response, your feelings about the event. Do you feel your ego fed, do you calculate the effects you hope to have had on this or that Friend (whether fearfully or with self-congratulation)? Were you too restrained from timidity, or just not inclined to exert yourself beyond a certain point? Are you surprised, worried about your reputation, or anxious about the implications or reception of your words?

Of course such things happen to us all from time to time—you are not alone. You keep close to the gift here, in the aftermath, by your inward posture during this time of review or reflection. This posture, or attitude, arises as you take care to cultivate a spirit of watchfulness, and the habits of mind and practice that support it. At first, you may need to devote a lot of attention to this "need" because you find it hard to do, so you must put energy, will, and perhaps thought or craft into doing it. You may also "need" to pay close attention because you are needy—fearful, prideful, too critical of self or others.

Yet it is important not to obsess or get lost in self-important self-scrutiny. If every event feels dramatic, dramatically good or bad, in your eyes, while it does not to others, you need to be cautious. It is a species of scruple to examine every event with fear. It is a species of pride to seek to read more significance into a thing than it warrants, or to over-dramatize your experience. Find the root, learn to name it, and then seek to face it down (a subject to which I return in more detail later). Understand where it has real meaning (as providing a warning to you), and where it is the expression of an aspect of self that is as yet unilluminated by Christ's teaching and guidance—that is, an aspect which you have not yet brought before Him openly and with confidence in his healing and instruction.

For the key to this sort of exercise is to submit your condition, with all its fears, ills, or confusions, to the work of Christ, as far as you understand it. To the best of your ability, look past your anxieties, fears, and analyses, until you have taken the time to sink down to the quiet, to come to the dwelling place of prayer. If, in your waiting, you still feel a great tension in your body, or your thoughts return to issues or arguments that insist on taking center stage, look at each of these things with love, until you feel them lose their grip on you. By "look-ing with love," I mean, acknowledge that they are real and important to you—don't think "I shouldn't be this way." Here truth is the path to progress in the spiritual life. If you need to, personify your besetting images, and assure them (or your-self) that they will receive their due, once you have come into the true quiet. "It takes its kingdom with entreaty, and keeps it by lowliness of mind."

It is most important for you to know first and foremost that you stand before the Lord as openly as you are able, and give yourself a moment (however long) to feel God's love, and your safety and dependence upon it.

Now you can take breath and then bring your issues for-ward, one by one. In that quiet place, you can be almost as undismayed by your disorder as God is. You can know, per-haps even with a certain rueful humor, that even if you could-n't admit your need, the Lord of counsel knows it. Hiding or dissembling is a pointless delay, really, and so the easiest thing to do is to bring the case forward into the light.

The lesson you are seeking to learn, till it becomes a set-tled, unquestioned reflex, is how to have a teachable mind. Thus, whenever you do a thing because you are called, or feel it is required of you, turn inward, and feel your condition. You will soon come to recognize, most of the time, when there is a major issue to address and when you can feel safe to move on without paying it much attention.

This can be put another way: learning from your gift as you act from it, you learn to be available and teachable as a habit. As a result the inward eye or ear opens more easily, and your mind is more and more illuminated by the mind of Christ. The goal here is to be open and watchful, trusting, and unforced. As Douglas Steere liked to quote, you ask "Was thee faithful? Did thee yield?" Sometimes the answer will be "No!" and sometimes "Yes!" In either case, by cultivating the habit I have described above, you will be able to give thanks in your confidence in the Lord's guidance, and make use of that guid-ance. If you don't ask, you won't learn.

15

On discouragement

You will often feel discouraged in your service. Highs and lows are a usual part of any spiritual life. Physical fatigue, oppressive weather, perplexities at work, unhappy news or difficult interactions, can cast you down. Further, events like these can be distracting from your spiritual practice, so that without your noticing it, you are not taking the time you usually do in prayer and devotional service, so that some accustomed spiritual nourishment is lacking, and your healthy rhythms are thrown off. If you are being very mindful of your spiritual health, and notice this kind of dryness, you may be tempted to treat it as more serious than it really is. If you re-establish your practice, a dryness due to such temporary causes will pass off quickly.

It is good not to think of one's faithfulness as depending upon "inspiration," in the common sense of that word. Typically, this implies a surge of energy and enthusiasm which makes things flow. There is adrenaline in it, and a sense of expanded possibilities. It does not last long; it is taxing on the body and the emotions, and soon runs out of steam, sapped by fatigue or opposition.

Of course, a minister may well have these moments of high energy and excitement, and they are not to be dismissed or devalued. They may be part of the movement towards an act of service, whether speaking in meeting or some other event requiring some risk. Nevertheless, they cannot be given more importance than they deserve. The "inspiration" you are after may include such moments, but will more durably consist in a sense of spiritual clarity, attention, and availability or presence to God and to those you meet.

But supposing that you have learned to look beyond these short-term changes in mood, sometimes you still will find yourself in a more extended time in which you feel disheartened

93

and weak. In such moments, the safest and the wisest path to insight is to sit down and wait to feel the Lord's presence before considering your condition.

This is not because sitting in the quiet will necessarily bring quick, specific consolation, or some magic answer. The important thing is first to reestablish your connection with your guide and counsellor. As Mary Capper wrote, "none has ever sought the Lord in vain, though He is pleased at times to hide the light of His countenance from His waiting, dependent children. In simplicity, humility and faith is our safety." (Capper 1860, 57)

You must begin by sinking down to where you can recognize God's presence, regardless of your feelings of unworthiness or restlessness. Be ready to see that some or much of your restlessness or sense of burden is really anger or frustration. Whether this is justified or not, it will need reckoning with. Seeking for the source must follow on recognition of your condition.

Be patient in seeking the place where you can feel the seed, because it is in this presence that you can do the work of understanding and responding to your discouragement. We are called upon to love the Lord our God with all our heart, soul, strength, and mind. It is only when we are at the place where we can feel God beloved, and ourselves loved in return, that we can undertake the prayer work needed to understand our condition. When we are in that place, we are likely to feel reassurance of our fundamental value as God's children. We are emboldened to look at ourselves in the truth, and made humble enough to take guidance, first from the Lord, and second from any of his faithful servants who may come to us with advice. I also find that it helps to recall the scripture here:

> fear not them which kill the body, but are not able to kill the soul;
> but rather fear him which is able to destroy both soul and body . . .
> Are not two sparrows sold for a farthing? and one of them shall
> not fall on the ground without your Father. (Mt. 10:28–9)

Even at our lowest and weakest, if our desire is to be faithful, God reaches to us even in our unfaithfulness or bewilderment.

Now, when you have found this place below fear and self-recrimination, you can begin to consider, in the light, the nature of your discouragement. As you seek for the answers, and use both mind and heart in the search, you will be able to recognize when you have found some of the truth. But do not rush to seize on the first thing that occurs to you, the first complaint you utter inwardly. At those moments, continue waiting in the light, letting any other complaints you may have, or other fears that you have felt, rise up into your consciousness. This will help you avoid premature conclusions, and premature closure to your inquiry.

Perhaps during this time, to spare your memory from too much work, you may wish to write your issues in a journal, or even on a piece of paper which you will discard once you are finished. The most important thing, however, is to stay in the place of quiet confidence, so that you need not fear anything that comes to mind. "The eternal God is thy refuge, and underneath are the everlasting arms." (Deut. 33:27)

It may be helpful to you to read some of the kinds of discouragement that other ministers have felt and struggled with. I have found that in considering these things, I sometimes have said, "Oh, that's what it is!" but just as often have said, "I am sure it's not one of these things, what else might it be?" and thus used these ideas as a way to push myself to seek harder for the sources of my own trouble.

Have you been unfaithful in some requirement?

This is a question that has much occupied ministers in all eras, however great their calling and their growth in the spirit. In fact, as you grow more practiced in listening for the Lord's voice, and feeling where his life rises in yourself and others, and greeting it with joy, you also become more aware of where this life is blocked, and especially where it may be blocked by your own deeds or attitudes. Certainly in my little measure, this one has cut deeply.

You may know very clearly that you have fallen short in something. In his essay "On being moved by the Holy Spirit to minister in public worship" Lewis Benson writes: "If the call is from God strength will be given. If not, the minister will feel a gentle rebuke and inner disquiet after he has spoken." Sometimes, another Friend will reinforce the message that the Lord has provided inwardly.

I remember one time when I had spoken in meeting, taking as my text the Lord's prayer. I sat down with a sense of disquiet, feeling that perhaps I had made a calculation that the message was required, rather than feeling led then to bring that matter to those present. Within minutes, a visiting Friend arose, and first quoted Cromwell: "In the bowels of Christ, think it possible you may be wrong." He then went on to quite a different message, very suited to the meeting's need, noting as he made the transition that he did not see the connection between the Cromwell quote and the rest of the message, but feeling sure he must say it. Who knows if he was led to this because I needed a rebuke? The outcome was that his words sharpened my attention to the inner rebuke I had felt, and I was able to learn my next lesson in discernment.

I would like to add here a passage from Joseph Hoag's journal:

> We were at Mamaroneck meeting. Here, finding my mind led into different subjects, I was thoughtful to close in good season; but after sitting down, I did not feel that clear quiet, which I commonly feel when I time it right; but being unwilling to rise again, or kneel—for my mind was arrested with both—I sat until it wore off, and then broke the meeting. After I got out, an elder came and took me by the hand, and said, "Joseph, thou has been preaching to others to be faithful to their gifts; hast thou been faithful to thine? I confess I did not expect the meeting to end so," and turned away. Though I did not expect to be found out in that way, I was glad to meet with such honesty from the Friend. (Hoag 1861, 153)

Of course, the unfaithfulness may not be in the line of ministry, but may be because of some act you took or neglected in your work or family life. The sense of reproach that arises from such an event can be troubling and distracting, and make you less able to sense where your path should go, and raise up emotional squalls and upheavals, so that your judgment is impaired, and your strength lessened, for a time. All of us are likely to have points on which we feel chagrin, regret, or shame, and which remind us that we have a way to go before we are really living from day to day, and hour to hour, in conscious awareness of God's presence. Furthermore, we must be alert to our share of the work of reconciliation in the world, and especially where we have some difference with another person, or a need to seek or give forgiveness.

> if thou bring thy gift to the altar, and there rememberest that thy brother hath aught against thee; leave there thy gift before the altar, and go thy way; first be reconciled to thy brother, and then come and offer thy gift." (Mt. 6:23–4)

Yet as you cast your mind about to see what might have been neglected, it is important not to seize on "the answer" too quickly. It may be that an idea that bears with it some weight of truthfulness is really only the door into your real trouble.

Do you feel that your work is not succeeding as you had hoped?

Especially when you have undertaken a concern which requires attention over some length of time, it is natural that you will not always feel happy with the results. Perhaps the service you offer is not encouraged, or is even discouraged. Perhaps you feel that Friends or others misconstrue your intent, your sincerity, your methods, or your competence; this is particularly painful if your home meeting is not able to support your concern, or engage with it seriously and respectfully. It may also be that circumstances seem to conspire against you; "way does not open," sometimes for a lengthy period of time. Then it is important to explore whether you are to remain committed to the concern, perhaps with a change of plans for action.

I am thinking of a friend who had received a powerful, clear leading to service in Africa—not to visit and preach, but to help build a new institution to serve the poor. So clear was it, that as she recounted the opening, it raised a sense of delight and inspiration in those who heard her tell the story. Yet as she moved forward in building the partnerships and collaborations that would make it possible to bring the help she was called to, more and more she encountered human obstacles. Others had agendas of their own; some suspected her motives; some feared that helping her would diminish their own status; some felt she should fit into some institutional structure that had no real room for her. How acute is the anguish when we meet such obstacles! How painful is it, to have something so beautiful treated as a suspect and maybe sordid matter! How long can the hope and tenderness continue before we start to ask: What really happened? Was it a motion of God's love, or just a good idea of our own, with no sense of divine life flowing in it, to open the paths to realization?

You may bring this to prayer, and to the advice of your Friends, and be guided to persevere, to wait with hope for the next way to open. This was my friend's experience.

Yet it is good to be willing to consider without fear whether your leading is being withdrawn. This may happen for reasons that have little or nothing to do with you. It needn't mean failure, but just that you have been as faithful as required. Another passage from Joseph Hoag is relevant here. In 1823, Joseph felt drawn to pay a visit to Friends throughout several yearly meetings. Because, he wrote, he had been active in the discipline, he had made some enemies, who then were not comfortable in supporting his leading:

> in so doing, I had offended so many, that they would not let me go. My Master returned the answer, "Do what I bid thee, and if I do not make way for thee, thou shalt be clear." (Hoag 1861, 249)

A final question to ask, however, is "Am I mistaken?" Tension between yourself and your community may be an indication that your friends feel a reluctance or resistance that is well-founded. If your words or actions cause dissension or division, or a feeling of scattering and depletion rather than one of gathering and opening into fresh life, then it is your friends' duty to address this simply, lovingly, and directly, and your duty to listen, in prayerful openness.

Do you feel that you are not getting the recognition or support that you deserve?

This is a feeling that is well known to anyone who strives to serve. Despite its commonness, however, it is something that is very hard to admit, and therefore it can be overlooked. Often when we are ashamed of a thought, we do not allow ourselves to honestly look at it. Here is one of the times when the light at work in us leads us to uncomfortable places, and shows us things we would rather not see.

It is important at such times to seek to the Lord for quietness of mind, so that you can reflect upon your feelings in a productive way. It is only once one has explored these feelings and their causes carefully that it is possible to move towards solution, or perhaps better said, towards freedom from them. But you cannot be free of them if you do not excise them at the root, and this may be long to seek.

It is hard sometimes to see what is one's right "status" in the community of God. Many a time, one can say to oneself, "He who would be greatest among you must become the servant of all," and know it intellectually. Yet being able to *feel* the rightness of it, and to dwell with the movement of love which enables one to serve as the Lord intends is not so easy to achieve. After all, the goal of such service is to enable one's brother or sister to live as a citizen of the divine commonwealth, and (as way opens) to nurture the life of Christ that is growing in them.

Just as great physical exertion requires rest and nourishment, so also faithful service of any kind does, as well. Yet it may be that we do not recognize when this reward and encouragement comes, or do not draw from it the real value it contains for us. Therefore, when you have acted on a concern, be on the watch, not only for inward confirmation that you did not miss your way, but also for the reward that comes as well. If you get in the habit of giving thanks as soon as you can, and accepting the sense of right action that comes after faithfulness, then you will in fact have much of what you need of recognition.

Although we can and should rely first and foremost upon God for sustenance, there are good reasons as well to want some human feedback, some assurance that you are in fact rendering service that has value. Our service is rendered for others, and in a social and psychological setting, which has its own truth to be considered. Yet sometimes we are alone, as far as human support is concerned. If the feedback does not come, yet it is clear that you are in your right place, then you must accept the sense of deprivation as also part of the ordering in which your service is enacted.

If upon serious reflection and prayer, however, the question is persistent, and makes you doubt your calling, then it is time to seek for guidance from your Friends. It may well be that your way is being shut up, that people are not receiving your services, and your inquiry will enable your advisors to explain if there is something you are doing which weakens your offering. On the other hand, your request for guidance may prompt Friends to recognize that they have been too backward in acknowledging their gratitude for your work, and encourage them to find appropriate ways to let you know that your service has been acceptable. For there is an art and skill to encouraging which we are not as quick to develop as we might be. I have found that, being a naturally reserved person, I did not really realize how little I did this, until it came before me in prayer, and I found myself encouraged to be more quick to affirm the good things that others have done, in a way that they can hear and take encouragement from. Inward good opinions sometimes are not enough to nourish a minister who is exerting herself, and perhaps at some real cost.

Do you feel that you need help, do not know how to proceed, or are facing an insuperable obstacle?

It very often happens that a Friend takes up a concern for some service, and gets along fine at first, but then obstacles arise. The way seems shut to us, or we feel as though our energy and optimism ebb away, so that we just can't seem to take the next step.

Part of our belief as Friends is that if we are following a true leading "way will open." When the way seems to close, our impulse is to question the leading, or our discernment about it at the beginning. Maybe I was just wrong about the timing, or the calling, or my understanding of the task; maybe my committee was not centered enough, or honest enough about their doubts. Something must be wrong.

Of course, something may have been wrong at that time of beginning. It may also be, however, that the material you are working with, the people or coalitions or the issues, are just extremely difficult, and will require persistence and a renewal of vision.

The journals are full of lamentations about how hard the work of the ministry can be sometimes. Sometimes the writer is clear that the meeting itself is hardened and unreceptive to the ministry being offered, which is, as Elias Hicks wrote more than once, "hard for the poor traveller."

The journal writers tend to seek for meaning in the sense of abandonment or hindrance, and sometimes these meditations are very useful to remember, even if your explanations might be couched in other language.

Job Scott, for example, was increasingly grateful to these times of trial, as they reminded him of the limitations of his own strength, and of the fact that his ministry was only in support of the inward work of Christ, whose life was seeking to gain its sway in the people. This helped him remember that he was only a servant, and if he was faithful in what he was given to do, nothing more was required, and he could take satisfaction that he was in step with the Guide.

> I travelled through many heights and depths in my own mind . . .
> and seemed to be the nearest losing all faith and hope in God,
> that I ever remembered to have experienced. I did not always
> abide sufficiently on the watch-tower, in confidence in him who
> has never failed me. (Scott 1831, 1:243)

Martha Braithwaite, wife of J.B., was active in the ministry in their youth, though less so as family demands increased upon her. In writing about a trip in the ministry to Ireland, she reflected upon why so often she felt caught up in the joy of acceptable service, and then fell into a time of emptiness and weakness. She thought of all the work she was doing during her travels, and "reflected that the vessel that is often in use must often be cleansed and returned to the shelf, ready for the next time," and thus saw that the swings of mood were in fact part of a larger whole, which was her being consistently ready during a time of intensive service.

Of course, you must seek in prayer for guidance, and also confide in a Friend or Friends whom you think may be able to listen effectively, and comment usefully. Be on the lookout also for unexpected guidance, as your inner debate or questioning continues. The most important thing is not to be hasty in judging what to do, either to press on or to give up. "Try the fleece wet and dry," especially if the leading seemed very clear, and was supported and affirmed by discerning Friends. Trust that original form of the gift, and in present difficulties be very reluctant to relinquish the sense of blessing that came with it. Especially if your present troubles have to do with arrangements and process, allow yourself to step back to pray in quietness of heart, indeed insist upon spending time in rest and prayer until quietness of heart returns, and remember that prayer is also action. You need to be free of the need to succeed, and even though longing to carry on, willing to stop—and vice versa. When you are really in that willing place where you can give thanks for what your portion is, you will be more able to take counsel and discern the next step.

Do you feel disheartened because people or ideas with which you are out of sympathy seem to be widespread or gaining currency?

In these times of cultural turmoil both inside and outside the Religious Society of Friends, you will sometimes encounter things that make you feel pain or even despair about what witness Friends may be making to the world. Your own preferred language and beliefs may be discounted or dismissed, and things you think of as being pivotally important seem of no importance to many others. Hearts will seem hard, or, even worse, indifferent to the deepest matters. This will tear at you. The more progress you make in your spiritual life, the more you are watchful for and obedient to the light, the more you will come to feel that spiritual dangers and openings are essential, and urgent. When things you find important are dismissed by others, and marginalized, the sense of pain and outrage can be very strong and persistent.

This has been the case in every age. It is no different now. Knowing this is only small consolation, since you will be feeling the temptations of anger or discouragement freshly for yourself. Yet the only safe path, the path that witnesses to the spirit of Christ, is one that bears with these things, and seeks in hope for the witness of God, which is unfailingly present to be reached to. I find at times like this it is valuable to meditate on the many messages contained within the well-known words of James Nayler, that sorely tried and faithful servant of Christ:

> There is a spirit which I feel, that delights to do no evil, nor to revenge any wrong, but delights to endure all things, in hope to enjoy its own in the end. Its hope is to outlive all wrath and contention, and to weary out all exaltation and cruelty, or whatever is of a nature contrary to itself. It sees to the end of all temptations: as it bears no evil in itself, so it conceives none in thoughts to any other. If it be betrayed it bears it, for its ground and spring is the mercies and forgiveness of God. Its crown is meekness, its life is everlasting love unfeigned, and takes its kingdom with entreaty, and not with contention, and keeps it by lowliness of mind. In God alone it can rejoice, though none else regard it, or can own its life. It's conceived in sorrow, and brought forth without any to pity it; nor doth it murmur at grief and oppression. It never rejoiceth, but through sufferings, for with the world's joy it is murthered. I found it alone, being forsaken; I have fellowship therein, with them who lived in dens, and desolate places in the earth, who through death obtained this resurrection and eternal holy life. (Nayler, in Drayton 1994, 76)

16

On where to seek discernment and guidance

Seeking counsel from other ministers

It is a matter for gratefulness that Friends have rediscovered the importance of eldership. However, nothing can take the place of the counsel and fellowship that ministers can offer to each other, and there is the greatest need for this kind of mutual cultivation and support. Indeed, the reason this book is being written at all is because such frank interaction among Friends in the ministry is so rare and precious, and this little book can at least offer an echo of it.

When a Friend is young in the concern, there is a lot to learn about knowing when to act or speak, and when to keep waiting. Those who have struggled with the same questions can offer support and advice that is grounded in personal experience. Ann Crowley describes how, while she was accompanying some Friends travelling in the ministry, she began to feel called to appear in the ministry. She held back, however, believing that she might be mistaken, and in any case her companions were more experienced and she should not get in their way. She kept silent, but they also did as well. She felt turmoil in her uncertainty, but

> I spent an instructive evening with my companions, who I believe were dipped into a sense of my condition. The next morning . . . [my] exercise was renewed; but I was still fearful of believing myself called to so great and important work, as to become a minister of the everlasting gospel of peace and reconciliation. (Skidmore 2004, 147–8)

She came to understand that her companions' silence was in fact a consequence of hers, that in those meetings she was given some service which would open the way for the others.

> This withholding more than was meet, appeared to shut up the way of my dear companions, for public labour. Indeed, I have

come to believe . . . that, in order to know the life and power to arise in our religious assemblies it is highly needful for all the living members of the body, to keep their ranks in righteousness, whether in doing or suffering for the sake of the cause. (Skidmore 2004, 147–8)

Other challenges arise, however, as one carries the concern for service through the ups and downs of life. In such cases, the sense of kinship and mutual responsibility between ministers can lead to real consolation as well as frank advice. Lydia Lancaster writes to an old friend,

> The last time I heard of thee it was a time of great weakness with thee, which took deep hold of my mind. . . . Maybe we shall see each other at our spring meeting, meanwhile let us be true in our desires for each other, and for Israel, and for the heritage of God everywhere, that Truth may increase, and cover the earth in a more general way to his praise, and the comfort of all his mourners, that they may put on the garments of praise, instead of the spirit of heaviness—so wisheth, so prayeth, thy firm friend and true lover in the covenant of endless life. (Skidmore 2004, 39–40)

It's not just at times of struggle and darkness, though, but also times of joy or solid accomplishment, that a word from someone you know to be an experienced colleague can confirm and solidify your experience. A few years ago, I found myself with a message breaking through with a fresh sense of freedom and fearlessness, to speak both more strongly and more tenderly from my inward experience than I had felt able to before. An older Friend said to me in an opportunity later, that he could confirm that he heard something authentic and fresh, and that I was finally "getting somewhere." Knowing his gift for listening, and his own long history of seeking for faithfulness, I was greatly encouraged—and put more on the watch than ever. When such a Friend says, "Thee was used, today," it is very meaningful; and it makes one more eager to affirm and encourage others.

But these personal encounters, important though they are, do not exhaust the resources that Quakerism has developed for the support of those carrying the concern for gospel ministry. A great service of the traditional meetings of ministers and elders was that they provided a regular opportunity for those under the same concern (each according to their own gifts) to speak to and guide each other. Where these meetings exerted control and repression, they were harmful, and no one would wish their return. Yet they had this virtue, that they were an explicit assertion by the Society that ministers sometimes should meet together for support and counsel.

In his article, "Our Quaker ministry twenty years after the cessation of recording," T.E. Harvey (of London Yearly Meeting) deplores the loss of the chance at yearly meeting for recorded ministers to meet and counsel with each other, which he found a great solace and help in his youth. It may be, however, that some will not have a clear sense of what kinds of advice he might have in mind when he writes:

> there are all kinds of simple, practical advice which those who are called to speak in meeting can offer to one another, and which cannot be given in the same way by those who never open their mouths in meeting and do not know from within what it means to do so. (Harvey 1946, 189)

It is also likely that such meetings could arouse concern or fear that they represent a potential "elite" within the larger body. Such fears can only be addressed by the experimental evidence of more humble, courageous, and effective service among those who attend and benefit from such gatherings.

> They were occasions in which experienced ministers, with great tenderness, and under the sense of a blessed unity in the love and service of Christ, often gave wise and helpful counsel to their younger brethren. Offerings in the ministry from those whose names were not yet recorded on the list of approved ministers were passed under review, in a confidential and loving spirit; and when occasion seemed to call for it, individuals were deputed to procure interviews with some of these Friends, and to convey to them messages of counsel or encouragement as the case might seem to require. (Dymond 1892, 15)

Perhaps more practical for modern unprogrammed Friends is the notion that ministers (which might mean "anyone who speaks in meeting and feels drawn to the gathering") should

gather together informally from time to time, for mutual support and advice. This kind of gathering is sometimes hard for
Friends to organize in their home meeting—perhaps because
of embarrassment, or some other sort of inhibition about naming gifts, or causing disagreements, or discomfort within the
community. For this reason, a concerned visitor is sometimes
better able to help this happen. Sometimes Friends in the
ministry were concerned to convene ministers either in their
home area, or when travelling. Such episodes are very common in the journals of the Quaker middle period, for such
Friends as Scott, Churchman, or Bownas, for whom this was a
perennial concern. From more recently, T. Harvey writes:

> I can remember attending in London some forty years ago [ca.
> 1900] the meeting of Recorded Ministers which was held at
> intervals . . . that is almost the only gathering of Friends engaged
> in the service of the Ministry which I can recall from my own
> personal experience, in spite of the very definite instruction of
> [London] Yearly Meeting encouraging everywhere this kind of
> fellowship. (Harvey 1946, 189)

Such gatherings were known from the earliest days of the
Quaker movement, and through meetings and correspondence, those Friends who bore some share of the ministry
trained, guided, encouraged, and reproved each other,
frankly and in love, for the work's sake. From the nineteenth
century, J. J. Dymond recalled the value of such occasions, and
urged their renewal in his own day:

> if something like the restoration of the "Preachers' meetings"
> which existed in the very early days of the Society could be brought
> about, it would be to me a joyful realization of the desire of many
> years . . . it is needless here to describe in detail what should be
> the duties of such meetings. They would . . . afford opportunity
> for united prayer, for considering the needs of the flock, and for
> taking counsel together in order to the furtherance and effi-
> ciency of the work of the Gospel among us. (Dymond 1892, 16)

I can relate the story of a recent, hopeful experiment in
this direction, which might help make this whole idea more
concrete, more realistic, and less forbidding than it might

appear to some readers of this chapter so far. In the 1980s and 1990s in New England, Friends who were travelling in the ministry met together three or four times a year, and communicated also by way of an occasional newsletter. These gatherings were quite informal, typically on a Saturday for a few hours; attendance varied from six or eight, to as many as 15. After some opening worship, we would spend the time it took to tell each other what we had been doing, where we had been going, interesting things we'd noticed at meetings we'd visited. In this way, we all improved our knowledge of events around the yearly meeting, and also became aware of meetings that were particularly in need of visits from Friends.

Many of us attending were not travelling much, or even were only thinking of doing so, and such Friends could hear all the different kinds of intervisitation that were going on, with or without minutes, with or without specific concerns or topics to talk about, and so on. We gave each other advice about travel minutes or questions about reporting to our own meetings, and gave each other feedback, and prayed for each other. We also found partners, made agreements to accompany each other, and shared potluck lunches and the stories of our everyday lives. The meetings faded away when several of the convening Friends were unable to continue scheduling meetings, and putting out newsletters. While they continued, however, they were instructive, refreshing, encouraging, and fun.

Reading the journals

[H]ow earnestly some of us have scanned the published biographies of ministers who have gone before us in search of such insight as we might there obtain into the way in which they have been led. How deeply interesting to us have been words dropped by living men and women who were treading the same path of service to ourselves—perhaps a little in advance of us—if therein we could find some hints for our own guidance or comfort? (Dymond 1892, 30–31)

Despite their healthy distrust of human reason and intellectualizing, Friends ministers have been drawn to read and study—the scriptures, of course, Friends' writings, but also (according to their inclination) history, philosophy, science, theology, and more. However, in addition to other material, I highly recommend a reading of the journals and other writings of Friends ministers from the past. These are our brothers and sisters, colleagues in the work, who have done their best to record their experiences as they have tried to live faithful to their concern for the people, both Friends and others.

When first I came among Friends, I was convinced by the life I felt in the meeting that I found. After a time, however, I was hungering for guidance that I was not able to get from the Friends surrounding me. I do not say they were unable to give it, but I did not know what I needed, and no one else diagnosed what was working in me, either, for quite a long time. I began to seek among Quaker writings for help, and twentieth century Friends, and George Fox, and these were not what I needed. When I encountered Howard Brinton's book *Quaker Journals: Varieties of Religious Experience among Friends,* I was made aware of a whole world of personalities whose testimony might speak to me.

I began with Woolman (always a good choice) and then found Samuel Bownas and Joseph Hoag. As I read their accounts, I profited from the sense of the deep work they were engaged in, and the sense that this engagement was under the influence of the Spirit of the Lord. When I spoke excitedly to him of the discoveries of insight and comfort I was finding in this reading, Ralph Greene, a Friends minister in Maine, said to me, "What you're dealing with here is a call to the ministry, that's all." I then went "to school" seriously with any records I could find of Friends who had grappled with this experience, both in the distant past, and more recently. Once my eyes were so opened, I was able to see more and more people whose words and lives could instruct me. While the words and example of living Friends are most precious, I recommend the reading of journals to any Friend, but especially to those who feel some stirring of a call to service in the gospel ministry.

The value of making "journal reading" a habit is that as your experience grows in the service your need for the good advice—and example—of other ministers does not go away, and your own experience allows you to see and hear things that would not have registered before. At first they may seem to be moving in a culture that is quite distant from yours, almost like scripture stories. Their experiences may seem distant and hard to grasp, and not only because of the language they use to describe them. As your service matures, however, you will come into a personal and vivid sense of much of what they describe. Sometimes it is easier when one is wrestling with new experiences or new questions to visit such counsellors, who do not demand interactions or conversation from the reader, and whose commitment and earnestness saturate their story-telling.

Elders

In recent years, as Friends have discussed what is necessary for vital meetings in these days, we have sometimes referred to the traditional roles labelled "minister" and "elder." We proceed best in considering elders when we remember that we are not talking about an abstract "job description" but rather individuals who are "well-grown in the truth," alert to the promptings of the inward monitor, and lovingly concerned for the meeting as well as for its members. What does "eldering" look like?

First a word about the institution of "elders." Early Friends assumed that persons of mature spiritual stature would be raised up under the Spirit's leading in their community, and like many other groups they adopted the term elder to describe such persons—a term that has good biblical roots. At the early stages of Friends, even into the eighteenth century, "elder" was a description of someone's condition, rather than an office to be filled. Thus, George Fox, the great example of the prophetic minister, was described as "that worthy elder in Sion," and so also were most of the publishers of truth at one time or another. However, from early times, it was recognized that there were people in each community whose spiritual qualities provided an anchor for the community life different from, and complementary to, what was provided by the publishers of truth. William Dewsbury as early as 1653 encouraged Friends to identify a few elders in each meeting, those "well grown in the truth." These Friends, who were experienced in the inward life, were the core of the meetings for business, which were at first not inclusive of all members of the meeting. (There was no formal membership then, hence the value of naming some who were recognized as being well settled spiritually).

The elders' functions were various, and as with ministers, there were no fixed roles to fill. They were the points of contact for travelling Friends; they arranged the holding of meetings, and had care for the right holding of the meetings for worship (then as now). Sometimes these Friends gathered for mutual support and counsel. Corresponding to the Second Day Morning Meeting of Ministering Friends in London was a biweekly meeting of men Friends not in the ministry.

It was in the 1690s, in Ireland, that we have the first records of elders as a specific office. Elders (a few in each meeting) were to be chosen, to meet separately from the ministers to consider the spiritual condition of the meeting. They were also to attend the meetings of ministers which had been held regularly for guidance, counsel, and refreshment from the earliest days of the movement. Thus began the trend that later became infamous for elders to exercise an influence counterbalancing that of the ministers in the leadership of the Society. In fact, formal meeting leadership evolved into a stable triad of contrasting or complementary roles: elder, overseer, and minister.

In the positive sense, however, the elders had essentially a nurturing role. One might say that their voice is embodied in our queries, for they were always to be asking questions: How is the meeting for worship? Do Friends have the ministry they need? Are the young being well-educated? Are you regular and punctual in attendance? Are Friends being buried, married, set up in business, and choosing their habitations after the manner of Friends?"

By the middle of the eighteenth century, the structure of meeting leadership had settled into a stable pattern that dissolved (along with so much else) during the course of the twentieth century. The ministers exercised charismatic authority; the elders exercised the authority of discernment; the overseers exercised the pastoral authority. The division of labor was thorough. For example, the Wilburite yearly meeting in New England recommended that an elder should have care of meeting and close it, to free ministers from the special attention that this duty should entail. More striking, if an elder began to speak in meeting, he/she was to suspend the exercise of eldership, and wait to see what his/her calling might be. There was little thought (at least in the discipline) that one might be both. While it seems unnecessarily rigid, it reflects the important insight that the kinds of inward work appropriate to each sort of service often are very different from each other.

The feeling we have now, looking back on that era, is that the ministers were the source of innovation and fresh leading— and sometimes error; the elders and overseers spoke for stability.[13] This is no more true than any such generalization—true in some cases, inaccurate in others. Certainly elders felt the need to provide stability and continuity during times of turmoil in the Society, and where powerful innovators arose, powerful personalities arose to resist them. The conserving role of the elders led to the negative connotations of the term "to elder."

Ministering Friends are easy to spot, part of their calling is to stand up and be heard. But it is hard to know how to nurture the birth and growth of elders, because they can so often

---

[13] This stereotypical tension is encapsulated well in the controversy over Job Scott's essay on "Salvation by Christ." Luke Howard, in writing that Job Scott was guilty of unsound doctrine in some of his writings, says, "There was certainly in the character of this dear Friend, a perceptible excess on the side of the imagination and the feelings. This had been the case with many good and useful men before him: and such a temperament makes a minister faithful, or courageous and energetic in the discharge of duty, but in measure disqualifies him from being a competent judge of doctrine and controversies." (Scott 1993, 70–71)

be unobtrusive. They are the quiet, thoughtful, prayerful Friends whose learning and inward growth do not stop, and whose care for the meeting grows as they grow.

A meeting's life needs guidance, stimulus, and cultivation—a healthy diet of several kinds of discipline. A loving elder (of whatever age!) can speak the hard truths of support and encouragement, and of restraint or even reproof, because we see how they love us faithfully. Of course, words are not needed, when the living is the message, and I know for myself that I have been learning the lessons of simplicity, directness, and simple prayer from some elders I meet who teach merely by their commitment to living Friends' understanding of the Gospel, in the inward life as well as the outward.

Always, Friends in the ministry, or others under a concern, have been encouraged to seek out a discerning elder or two, who should listen with sympathy and honesty to the concern. Not all concerns should be followed, or followed right away; not all should be followed by the one who first perceives the need, or in the form that first appears. An elder who has had experience with many Friends, and who has maintained an inner watchfulness, provides a powerful connection with truth for the minister or other Friend in the turmoil of leading, confusion, or temptation. A Friend can better open him- or herself to the sense of divine power, and dare to take risks in service, knowing that wise, concerned Friends (whether elders or ministers) will understand, advise, encourage, and restrain in love and honesty as needed.

17

On being dipped into sympathy

Friends traditionally have used the word "baptism" or "being dipped" in many senses, but very often it connotes a journey of spirit into deep and vivid sympathy with the condition of a meeting or individual. While at times this happens in an unexpected or spontaneous fashion, often it comes as one result of an exercise in prayer about the person or meeting in question. When you come to realize that you have been brought by the presence and power of the Spirit into this sympathy with another, it may lead you to more purposeful or directed prayer, as the inner exercise makes you alert to issues about which the sympathizing Friend is exercised.

> [T]o visit the immortal life, where it lies, requires great abstractedness of mind. . . . Oh! sometimes when in this situation, how clearly has the state of meetings and individuals been opened, to my mind, as plain as ever I saw the face of another with my natural eyes! (Grubb 1863, 39)

Often, ministers feel such a concern for others in the ministry, and part of maturing as a Friend is being alert to opportunities to act on that concern. It often seems to me that we too rarely offer a word of encouragement or thanks. I have on more than one occasion been lifted up out of a feeling of spiritual fruitlessness when a Friend happens to speak of some way I've been helpful, often years before. A story told about J. S. Rowntree illustrates both this practice, and the way that loving concern should be yielded to:

> His own share of ministerial service gave him a deep sympathy with that of others, both older and younger, and he did not fail to show it. An esteemed minister was visiting York on religious service . . . under a secret feeling of deep inward discouragement. . . . With sympathetic insight, [Rowntree] had probably divined her depress, and it nerved him to break through his natural shyness and reserve, and to tell her how, years before, in a

"family visit," some words of hers had gone home to his heart with helpful power, and been just the message he needed. As she listened her sadness and depression passed away, and she entered the meeting with a song of rejoicing in her heart, strong once again to do her part. (Doncaster 1908, 25)

Thus, the first need is to listen sympathetically, and with an intent to support the other: "Prove all things; hold fast to that which is good." (1 Thes. 5:21) A Friend moved by concern may sometimes be required to offer advice or reproof, when it is felt that the other was not being faithful.

Edward Hicks described how, when a young minister, he was reproved publicly by an elder. Meekly but firmly he accepted any rebuke that applied, but asserted that he still felt that he was not in the wrong. He reports the comment of an older minister at that point:

> Thomas Scattergood then spoke nearly in the following manner: "I rejoice, Friends, that this matter has taken the turn that it has. I was sorry for the interruption, and felt much for the young man, who I saw was a stranger. I thought that he had got a little lost, and I was travelling with him in spirit, to find a safe landing place." (Hicks 1851, 60)

A well-known case is that of David Ferris, who was prodded in this sense by the aged and experienced Comfort Hoag to recognize and act upon the responsibility that was dawning on him:

> [While accompanying Comfort and her companions as she was visiting my area] I attended a meeting with them, in which I felt a concern to speak to the assembly, but, as usual, evaded it. After meeting Comfort said to me, "David, why didst thou not preach today?" I . . . endeavored to appear innocent and ignorant of any concern of that kind. . . . On the following day, a similar concern came upon me, and I evaded it as before. After meeting, Comfort again said to me, "David, why didst thou not preach today?" I endeavored to pass it by as I did before; but she said it was not worth while to evade it, for she was assured that I ought to have preached that day, and that I had almost spoiled her meeting by refraining, which had hindered her service. (Grundy 2001, 52)

When he finally gave in to the call to speak (he had by this time been resisting all such concerns for twenty years), Comfort came to him and said,

> her anxiety for my deliverance from that bondage was such that she was willing to offer up her natural life to the Lord, if it might be a means to bring me forth in the ministry; and that on making the offering I rose to speak. (Grundy 2001, 53)

This kind of experience is known today, for sure, and occasionally described, especially when Friends are discussing the spiritual interplay between ministers and elders during intervisitation, when anxiety and the sense of demand and focus are heightened. Yet it often enough happens in a weekly meeting for worship, and I have more than once been made strongly aware of the condition of a Friend, either present with me in the same meeting, or at some distance, whose feelings and needs are perceptible as I sit in waiting worship— and so my own needs have appeared as well to others.

This sensitivity can also play an important part in the good order that arises under the guidance of the Spirit during worship, when there may be several Friends present who are feeling the meeting's exercise. Then it is especially good for each Friend who feels drawn to stand and speak, to cast about one more time, to feel whether someone else should instead stand at that moment. The discernment about this can be made easier if the Friends who have care of meeting are not punctilious about closing by the clock, but wait to allow the meeting's exercise to reach a good stopping place.

Job Scott describes his own thoughts on this matter of getting in each other's way:

> It may be that I stept into the service of some other exercised instrument. For I am convinced that there is such a thing, as having so much feeling sense of, and sympathy with, another's exercise, as to make great caution necessary, lest we move in each other's commission, without a real commission of our own . . . thou mayst feel thy spirit dipped into a near sympathy with the exercise of another who is under the qualifying hand, and just ready to move in the strength and clearness of a right commission.

And if thou art not strictly careful to wait for a clear opening, thou mayst move in a feeling of another's exercise, to thy own hurt, the hurt of that other instrument who was receiving the commission, and even to the great hurt of the whole meeting. And in thy missing thy way, and running before thy guide . . . thou wilt retard thy own progress in the right way. . . . But if thou art always careful to wait for a right commission, and never to move without it, thou wilt never thus err from the right way, but will surely be preserved. (Job Scott 1831, 1:232)

Of course, the sympathy that one feels may not be related to speaking in meeting. You may be given a clear vision that a particular Friend should be encouraged about some other concern, and while it is natural to be tentative about announcing this sense (since we can be mistaken easily enough), it is also good to act, however cautiously, on the sensation, because you may well have been made aware of another's situation at a crucial moment. Acting in concern, with due care, will provide you with some experience and wisdom about the accuracy of your discernment.

18

On being in your own meeting

If you have a sense of calling to the ministry, then you are presented with a problem by your faithful attendance at your home meeting. How often should you speak? What danger is there in speaking often in your meeting? It is true to say, "Keep close to your gift, and speak only when called," but frankly being in your own meeting may introduce considerations that make this discernment rather difficult.

For one thing, speaking in meeting for worship on First Day is the main "outlet" that seems to be available to Friends with a calling. If you think that First Day meetings at home are the only place to exercise your gift, then you will exert much time and effort, indeed feel much anxiety at times, in trying to figure out if you should speak, every time you go to meeting. This is especially true if you are new to the calling—as I can attest to from my own experience.

We do not often sit in families, have appointed meetings, travel under concern, and have much worship in our meetings for business. With valuable exceptions, our practice in that sense is impoverished, and the openings when ministry might be called for are very few. A person with a real calling who exists in a Quaker culture that is so very constricted may very well feel more pressure to speak at meeting than might really be right to yield to.

There is both a problem of ego, and also a problem of stewardship here. If you have a calling, and you don't exercise it, how can you tell you have the calling after all? From the point of view of ego, speaking in meeting can become important for self-validation. This problem may be most acute if you are just coming under a sense of particular concern for the ministry, and needing the sort of guidance and affirmation that outward action can elicit. The issue of stewardship arises from a kindred anxiety to be as faithful as possible, which can be construed to mean "be as active as possible."

Another source of tension (and temptation) may arise because you may be operating upon a theory that meetings need a certain quantity of ministry, and if no one else will offer it, you need to. The pull to speak may be especially strong in a meeting that is weak—because it is dwindling, or because it is new and small, or because it has few experienced Friends, or because it has lost its way and become drowsy and shallow. A concerned Friend who is sensitive to the silent indicators of a meeting's health will feel these conditions of weakness very acutely, and just on that basis will want somehow to respond constructively.

I have felt that pressure very strongly in very small meetings, where the sense of spiritual life was flickering out, and the only, rare vocal exercise that happened was stereotyped, or didn't seem grounded in spiritual experience, however thoughtful it might be in other ways. At times in such conditions, I have spoken in the hope that a new voice might encourage these Friends to look to their own responsibility more, and take more part. There are very many meetings in which faithful ministry can play a valuable role in building up the life from a low point, and if you have a very strong sense that the meeting is passing through a time of need, this may be a stimulus to be more watchful for authentic leadings to speak, and more watchful in times of prayer between meetings.

I don't believe I did much harm in times when I spoke from anxiety rather than from a real spiritual motion within the meeting. However, I believe that at such times my activity was a merely human gesture, which probably did not add any positive quality to the meeting's spiritual practice, but left it in the shallows. When I have offered ministry that was too superficial, it may have encouraged others to speak too easily, and too much from the head or the heart, rather than the Spirit's teaching. Some people offer messages that are drawn from their own thought, and shy away from claiming any divine impulse to speak, and yet make their offerings with good intention, and they form part of the meeting's teaching ministry. A steady diet of this, however, is not healthy for a meeting, and it can become so if the concerned members feel too strongly the need for words.

Sometimes people make a good beginning, gain a sense of confidence and helpfulness, and then giving themselves too much credit, speak in meeting as a way to establish their own importance, or as a way to honor encouragement that has been given. This is human, easy to feel, and poisonous if it is not recognized and expunged promptly.

> I believe that some of us are tempted to think, that unless we appear to take some active part in truth's service, we may be looked upon by others, and perhaps by ourselves, as useless, lifeless members; but far otherwise is my judgment at this time. The humble, patient traveller, who bears the burden of the word, until the right time comes for deliverance (when the message will be accompanied by a measure of power and authority), assuredly works essentially for the general good. (Capper 1860, 53)

Now, it seems to me that for someone just coming into a sense of concern and deeper commitment, speaking in one's home meeting is a safe way to go to school. It is there that you are most likely to get honest encouragement or restraint, given in love and real knowledge. If the messages offered are not arrogant, too intellectual, or combative—if discerning Friends feel that you mean well, and are not merely affirming yourself—then the meeting will hold what is good, and gently encourage it, and their love, prayers, and comments will help you learn your way, understanding what your gift is at the time, and what is not really called for. The Advices down the centuries have from time to time encouraged forbearance on the inexperienced and over enthusiastic whose intent is good, but judgment unformed.

Over-frequent speaking also can arise naturally enough from a surfeit of new discipline. If you are feeling drawn in your devotional practice to more Bible reading, for example, or grappling with the roots of the peace testimony or some other great issue that engages your mind and heart, you will be filled with ideas and excitement, and your spirit will be cultivated. It may very well be that this should find its way into ministry—but not necessarily now, and not necessarily while it's most fresh in your mind!

Everyone who speaks in meeting more than a few times a year will speak more often sometimes, and less often others. It is good to monitor that in yourself, and ask yourself if you perhaps are too eager, too accustomed, or too needy when rising. Some people speak more when they are under some inner work or trouble. It is good if we can come to see that this is true, and that we are seeking comfort for ourselves, rather than speaking for the meeting's help. Not that these are mutually exclusive! It may be that the ministry that you need to hear can sometimes come through your own service.

Some Friends rightly speak often in their own meeting, serving Friends there humbly and simply. If to the very best of your understanding you are really being led to speak very frequently, however, then it is good to consider whether you should perhaps be travelling, because you are being worked upon very intensively by the Spirit, and the concern may be not just for your home meeting. Here is where consulting with your advising Friends will be important, because in wrestling with such questions, it is very easy to mislead yourself. It is for the good of the meeting as well as your own service that you should take care about over-frequent "appearing" in the ministry.

It is impossible to lay down hard and fast rules, however. Just remember Bownas' admonition, that the minister should not think that he (she) must always be doing something around meeting. I leave this section with a quotation from Penn's *Rise and Progress*:[14]

> if therefore it was once a cross to us to speak, though the Lord required it at our hands, let it never be so to be silent when he does not. (Penn 1980, 69)

---

[14] Of this booklet, John William Graham said, when delivering the Swarthmore lecture on Quaker ministry, that in 1691 Penn had already written the Swarthmore Lecture on ministry. Pages 65–85 in the Friends United Press edition are delightful, wise, moving, and in Penn's most lucid and winning style.

Having said this much on some matters of judgment, let me return for a moment to an encouragement to move beyond our conventions. The more Friends feel open to, and indeed eager for, worship in many places, and diverse times, and for shorter or longer periods of time, the better for us all. While I recommend this as a generality, it is also a key point for the health of your ministry, and for the renewal of a living ministry among Friends. Therefore, it is good to be open to the possibility that you are called to other kinds of service than in First Day worship.

The important point is that the minister, who is on the watch for motions of the Spirit to encourage, may become aware of an opportunity to serve at any moment, and in a variety of ways. It may not be in delivering a message in meeting. It may be in speaking to someone at a moment of tenderness and accessibility, or doing some simple act of material service for them. It may be dropping into a short period of prayer while travelling to work, or otherwise going about your daily business. In this way we can learn to become more fully aware of the presence at every step, and in every situation. Living in this awareness is the source of nourishment and prophesy to our selves and our times, when there is a desperate famine of hearing the words of the Lord. (Amos 8:11) It may be yielding to the sense that it is now urgently time to write to someone, thank them, or spend time thinking out a problem that has burdened us somehow, and now suddenly is ready for solution.

Finally, it is a real contribution for every minister (like every member) to take part in our meeting for discipline, committees, and other meeting work as reverently, humbly, and alertly as possible, and thereby even if we are silent, we help others participate in depth. This is also a necessary part of your spiritual schooling, as it opens new ways to see the life of Christ at work in your fellow-members, or inhibited in them, and to learn from them.

Many of these actions will be invisible to anyone's sight, but they are part of the work as much as the act of speaking. They are part of our experience of the Spirit, which we are given both for its own sake, and possibly also for others'—if we digest them correctly—so that when the time is right they temper or color or enrich our service, or make our speaking more truthful and more faithful. As Joseph Hoag wrote, "Preachers have a need to learn as well as teach." (Hoag 1861, 342)

19

On listening to the ministry of others

As you become more intentional about a concern for the gospel ministry, you may become more vulnerable to the tendency to focus on your own speaking or not speaking in meeting, and less focused on the prayer that the Gospel be preached to and in the hearts of those present. So an important thread in your prayer during the week, and when you sit down in worship with your Friends, is the longing that whether in words or through the silent operation of God's Spirit, Friends are instructed, opened, led, comforted, as they need.

As part of this earnest prayer for the prosperity of gospel life, you should also pray that the right people be led to speak if that is called for, and to support them with your attention, charity, and love when they appear. In this connection, it is good to seek to be more and more attentive to the ministry of others, praying that it be fruitful in the lives of the hearers, and exerting yourself more to see how it may instruct or nourish you. In addition, it is sometimes possible to follow along with those who are offering ministry, as you support them in prayer. As illustrated in the previous chapter, Friends have often been able to feel when someone has been too timid, holding back, or wandering too far from their leading.

This sympathy, and desire for the welfare of the meeting and those ministering, can make you more ready and insightful in giving encouragement and fellowship. You will also profit from learning more about the many forms of gift that are poured out upon the people. It may lead to instructive conversation and mutual guidance.

Samuel Bownas wrote about how he and his friend Isaac Alexander, who came into the ministry at the same time, had gotten back together after a time of separation, and observed that each had grown in their gift:

We were glad to see each other, as well as to hear each other, which when we did, it appeared to me that Isaac was improved considerably, and he said the same of me, observing that I preached the practical doctrine of the Gospel he thought, more than he did; for his preaching was very much in comparisons and allegories, which he apprehended were not so plain and easy to the understandings of the vulgar, as what I had to say. We had now an opportunity of opening our minds to each other. (Bownas 1839, 8)

There is a possible risk, however, which is that listening carefully and attentively you may see things in another's gift which make you discount your own gift, and wish that you had his learning, her eloquence or ability in expounding scripture, use of humor, etc. The other Friend may seem to be better accepted, more sought after, speak with more authority, somehow be more accomplished. Even to state such feelings is to see clearly how petty and unworthy they are—yet they do occur, especially if we are in a time of uncertainty or difficulty, and we are seeking to be as serviceable as possible in the work. The only possible recourse is to be frank with yourself and God. Remember God's love and forgiveness, and wait patiently until you can feel the pure and sweet gift of the divine presence, freeing you from the worries and discomforts that your own self-judgment bring to you. Then wait for a renewed sense of what you personally are called to right now.

20

On passionate attachments

While the path of spiritual growth should be a journey towards greater integrity of the personality, this integrity comes step by step. Often, our spiritual growth is slow or at a standstill, and we await something that can precipitate a breakthrough. We may well be unaware that we have come to a period of stagnation, so when the breakthrough comes, it adds the power of surprise to the excitement of awakening, and our first sensations are those of warmth and expansiveness. If we come to this breakthrough because of a personal encounter, the person may be very much a focus of our attentions, and recipient of the warmth to an inappropriate degree.

I am speaking in very general terms, because this kind of experience has more than one form. The minister is as liable to such confusions as anyone else, and yet has more reason than most to be aware of them, and to look past them, because it distracts you from listening to your Guide. It can take the form of a passionate attachment to a party or faction, for example, so that your judgment is ceded to the group, and under its spell you come to hold opinions of issues, people, and events merely because these are the opinions or policy of the group.

Very often, however, it takes the form of passionate attachment to a person, whose voice, words, example, or personality somehow have touched you and awakened you, so that you feel opened and more lively, optimistic, motivated, committed. In many cases, this does little harm, and even much good, and the initial intensity passes off soon. But it can in fact do great harm under some circumstances. Here I will address two forms this can take: hero-worship and sexual attraction. Ministers may be the object or the subject of either of these; the way they respond may have important consequences for their own spiritual well-being, and for that of the other person involved. A determined focus on clarity, purity, and stillness is necessary as the foundation for a constructive response to this powerful, ambiguous, but creative experience.

Hero-worship

Perhaps this is more common for young people, but some personalities are liable to it at any age; I believe this is true of myself. Someone who has force of personality and insight may have just the characteristics to engage, awaken, challenge, and inspire someone, and they seem to embody a whole course of study in themselves. The feelings, entirely natural and in a sense commonplace, can be quite strong, especially if the "hero" seems to have been the catalyst for the solution of an important problem, or a particular source of solace. Speaking in uncharacteristic mood (as far as we know) and in the idiom of another time, here is James Nayler writing to George Fox in 1653:

> My father, my father, the glory of Israel, my heart is ravished with thy love above what can be declared . . . within this month I have suffer[ed] much; since I heard of thee my heart is filled with love. Pray for me my dear; they are for blood in this place, but the living truth spreads abundantly, praises forevermore. (Nayler 2004, 2:577)

When you are caught up yourself by a person who has such an effect upon you, if you retain your own bearings, and in the light seek to incorporate what the "hero" has enabled you to see as nourishment for your own search, then the experience is a real blessing. In fact, the act of centering into the Lord's presence, and then giving thanks for the person and their effect upon you is a way to move beyond the personal, and begin to separate what is in the life from what is more temporary, without despising the human feelings involved.

It may happen that you yourself engender that sense of excitement for someone else, and you may become aware of it. Then it is good to remember the phrase, "nursing father (or mother) in Israel," (Is. 49:23) and your calling, which is to love, honor, and encourage the divine life in others as you are able. A passage from Catherine Phillips is very eloquent on this point:

> When we are singularly made instruments of good, in the hands of Providence to any soul, there is a natural aptitude to lean a little to the instrument, and to prefer it above others, which may for a time be allowable. The Lord, leading the mind by gradual steps from the love of other objects to the entire love of himself . . . may permit it for a season to lean to an instrument; in which case a prudent reserve is necessary, as well as a tender regard to the growth of the party thus visited. (Catherine Phillips, in Skidmore 2003, 76)

Sexual passion X SIN OF LUST

The rush of warmth engendered by an experience of spiritual intensity may take quite another form. Perhaps the best way to put it is that such moments of opening make us very aware of someone on many levels, and this may include the level of sexual passion. Logan Pearsall Smith writes with asperity about his charismatic father's unfortunate affair with a woman who attended one of his revival meetings:

> [N]ature, in one of her grossest economies, has placed the seats of spiritual and amorous rapture so close to each other that one of them is very likely to arouse the other. Even the holiest of saints and most devoted of nuns—so exactly do these two forms of ecstasy feel alike—have sometimes found it extremely difficult to distinguish between them. . . . When a holy preacher sat near a sanctified sister, or a female penitent close to her confessor, they became more conscious of the Baptism of the Spirit; and as my mother sardonically expressed it, the nearer to each other they sat, the deeper and richer this consciousness became. (L. P. Smith, in West 1990, 378–9)

In a way, this hardly seems worth remarking upon, since it is a commonplace of church scandals from any century. Yet it is important to name it in this book, because it is a phenomenon that is common enough among Friends, even when we minimize the importance of charismatic leadership. If in unprogrammed meetings we do not have people whose attractiveness is amplified by microphones and high production values seen in some evangelical settings, we do have a practice which fosters and values intimacy and openness, and is quick to take note of a sense of passionate engagement in spiritual matters. Radiant people are attractive to others; a Friend who is sharing with intensity about his or her inner life is radiant. So also is a Friend who listens openly and with a real sense of focus. The initial response to that radiance may feel like the beginning of a love relationship, and so both parties are vulnerable, because the signals being sent are often exchanged at an unconscious level, and engage one or both before they are aware. There is warmth, and delight, and a sense of fitness and expansion, which are natural and powerful, and can open paths that are better not to walk.

This is not a feature peculiar to recent times, when the "hedge" of formality and Quaker protocol has been removed. We can quote Catherine Phillips again, cautioning "young women in a single state, who travel in the service of the ministry" with words that apply to either sex, of any age:

> [they should] guard their own minds, lest they admit of any pleasing imagination, and stamp it with the awful name of revelation; and so slide into a familiarity and freedom of conversation and behaviour, which might tend to engage the affections of young men. Secondly, [they should] endeavor to retain a feeling sense of the state of the spirits of those with whom they are intimate . . . so will they be the better able to judge of their motives for accompanying them, or of any other act of kindness; and may wisely check any forward thought which looks beyond friendship. (Catherine Phillips, in Skidmore 2003, 76)

The challenge is always to accept the positive value of such openings, and in a sense choose from among the many strands of feeling, to encourage those which promise true spiritual growth. This requires of the minister considerable self-awareness and tact. Withdrawal or distance may be called for in some cases, but most often a careful attention to limits is enough to establish the relationship on a safer footing. Phillips writes:

> I confess, it is sometimes a nice point, to be ready of service to such [as feel personal attachment too strongly], and preserve

the unity of the spirit, free from a mixture of natural affection; a distinction which I fear has been overlooked by some to their great hurt, but which truth, if adhered to, will make; and will also direct to steer safely betwixt these dangerous extremes. (Catherine Phillips, in Skidmore 2003, 76)

Any public Friend is likely to have encountered such an emotional situation. Most negotiate it appropriately. Some, however, do not. In such a situation, it is critical to remember that you are an emissary, a servant carrying out a task, and that if you have been faithful up to that point, part of what has opened up the feelings of the other is the sense you convey of the reality of the presence, and the beauty of that Spirit by which you have been led. If you do not remember that, and do not feel a concern not to dishonor the claim to service and calling that brought you there, then you do great damage to the spiritual life of yourself, the person you become involved with, and any who become aware of the situation.

It is important to be clear about the source of the damage: it comes because you take a thing that is claimed to have a divine element, and make it a matter of human emotion. There is nothing wrong with falling in love, and there is nothing wrong with the prior process whereby, in a time of spiritual openness and trust, one person becomes very open and drawn to another. The wrong comes from not distinguishing the motives at work, from the temptation to deceive self or other, and from not recognizing that, if intense emotions are awakened, one's ability to discern is likely to be quite impaired. When such situations arise, it is very painful to speak about, and Friends are reluctant either to raise the issue to a valued friend, or have the concern voiced with reference to themselves. See chapter 23 below, "On opportunities: part 2."

I believe that travel, to other meetings or large gatherings like yearly meetings, the Friends General Conference Gathering, or Friends United Meeting triennials, are times when this kind of confusion is even more likely than in one's home meeting. When travelling, there is the natural fact that you are outside the constraints and stresses of everyday life;

and encounters with new people draw us out and stimulate us. There is also a tendency when travelling to be at one's best—in fact, if you have yielded to a leading to travel in the ministry, it often happens that you reach a state of coherence and interior clarity that is not always your condition under normal circumstances, and is in a sense a special gift arising from your focus on the service. If you recognize that your journey has helped provide an unusual time of spiritual focus, and keep yourself carefully centered, this focus experience may well be an opportunity of growth and guidance for you. This humility, in addition, can serve to help discernment if you find someone being drawn to you at this time of intensity and openness.

None of this is unique to the travelling Friend, but the informality and naturalness of our interactions, the value we place on leadings and feelings which may have many sources, our lack of formality about oversight and support for Friends travelling under concern—these bring additional reasons for caution.

In the end, the fundamental point is, remember whose you are, and for whom you are empowered to be at work.

21

On "bearing the burden" of a concern

A concern or leading is evidence of God at work among us. Concerns can be large or small, short or long, private or public. They can be the impulse to speak in meeting on Sunday, or to write a letter to your senator, or to undertake work within your community on race-relations, or to take better care of your health. If they come with the sense of divine requiring, what could be more important, more awesome, more confirming?

There are occasional stories in the journals in which a "burden" on a minister is not approved by a meeting, and the minister "leaves it with the meeting" to carry. For example, from Joseph Hoag's journal:

> I found my mind impressed from day to day with a prospect of paying a religious visit to the inhabitants of Nova Scotia and the adjoining British Provinces, and to Friends with others, generally in New England. After considering the importance of the subject for several months, the Lord gave me to see clearly that the time was come to inform Friends of my concern, which I complied with at the next monthly meeting, under a feeling sense of the greatness of the undertaking. The meeting took up the subject and appointed a committee . . . they kept it along about one year without giving a decided report. At length the concern left me, as though it had never been; of this I informed the meeting. It seemed to shock the Friends who had held back; the business dropped here. I felt no more of it for more than a year, being quite easy; but those Friends who held back, were much uneasy the whole time. (Hoag 1861, 78)

Again, Edward Hicks describes a time when he comes across an isolated Friend, long out of contact with a meeting, and clearly not very religious. Hicks asks him, as the only Quaker in the region, to arrange to invite people from the area to a meeting. The local Friend professes no interest in helping, and dismisses them rudely. Hicks's companion then says "We do not wish to put thee or anybody else to any trouble or inconveniences, and are only sorry that Friends . . . should be so mistaken in their man. We will therefore bid thee farewell, and pass on." Hicks writes,

> My friends then arose from their seats to depart, when the old man replied in substance, Stop, stop, this won't do, you are not going to throw the responsibility of the concern on my shoulders. I can't submit to it; I must see if the Methodists can't accommodate you; they like preaching as well as any. (Hicks 1851, 79)

At first there is something very mysterious in this kind of story. Yet further reflection reveals some of the understanding that lies behind it. First, Friends then (and now?) believed that if a Friend felt a concern to undertake religious service, it might well be God intervening in history, just as in former days God sent the prophets and apostles off on missions. Second, since Friends believed that the meeting should test to see if this was a true leading or not, the meeting shared the responsibility for the ministry, a responsibility that was not abstract. Woe to the meeting if it blocked the authentic motions of the Spirit! Clearly, in the story from Edward Hicks, even the skeptical old Friend who had no use for preaching still felt some residual reverence for the minister's concern, and saw it as something requiring responsible care.

An additional dimension has to do with the way a community accepts concerns in its midst. In accepting a minister's concern, if it is in right ordering, the meeting is opening itself to spiritual gifts of several kinds. It is encouraging one of its members to be faithful to the Spirit's guidance, and not hold back. It is enacting its faith that the Spirit pours out gifts for the good of the people, and that the meeting and the individual jointly can sense and accept these gifts, and take good care of them, however large or small they might be. No one might predict the good that might come from Joseph Hoag's faithfulness—the encouragement, the enhancement of spiritual health, the good example he may set for others, the comfort and guidance he may be able to offer, and not least the learning and spiritual growth that will come to him if he is faithful.

All these constitute real values, spiritually speaking, which are at stake in the response to the "burden" that the minister feels, and shares with the meeting. It may be right for the meeting to say "No, we are not clear for you to go," but it is good for the meeting to do it knowingly. This is also why it is so important for meetings to be constructively and prayerfully involved in the support of concerns: it may open the way to more abundant life for one or for many.

One final reflection: in providing oversight for Friends under concern, it is all too easy to talk about logistics, or about the Friend's experiences to date, or his or her emotional condition or perplexities, in a way that is humanly warm and supportive, but disconnected from the concern itself. Caught up in the experience of the work, and the personalities and events of it, the ministering Friend may sometimes not be able to keep the core of the concern in mind. The support committee, or you as a sympathizing friend, must preserve the presence of mind enough to make sure that the context for all the necessary, natural, and fascinating conversations always be the care and stewardship of the concern itself: Has it changed? Do the difficulties or opportunities that the Friend relates look different if the original concern is recounted? Is there something being overlooked?

This may seem to go without saying, but I believe it does not. Often enough I have seen something like the following (a slightly disguised blend of two true and recent stories). A Friend had a concern to service in a developing country; the calling came with a lot of purity and urgency, at an opportune but surprising moment in her life. Way seemed to open marvelously to find funding, advice, and allies, and the clarity of the concern was evident to her meeting and support committee. Furthermore, as she followed the concern, she found new gifts she did not know she had, or had not understood before; and her faith, that is, her reliance on God's guidance, was strengthened. As she went ahead with the concern, she encountered problems: aspects of herself that needed to be transformed or healed, logistical challenges unforeseen, and mixed motives among her allies, so that she could not be sure what the meaning was of commitments and promises made to her, apparently in support of her work.

Naturally enough, when the outward conflicts and the inner doubts rose to a high enough level, the Friend was frozen from moving forward, not wishing to do wrong or to keep at a hopeless task, and not free of the leading to help. When her committee met with her, the natural inclination was to follow up the details of the issues, discussing them and making sense of them; this kind of reflection was definitely needed. Yet if unchecked, it would tend to stay at the level of personalities and motives, strategies and tactics. In fact, while these might be helpful, they were also in some ways confusing to the Friend in travail, because this level of discussion focused on specific actions and their consequences. This can be like stepping from one room into another: the original context is left behind, and if you keep moving to the next room and the next, that origin is harder and harder to return to, and the frames of reference shift further and further from the entry point. A Friend on the committee realized how the conversation was drifting, and said, "Wait a minute. Let's return to your original concern. Can you describe it again, just as it came to you? That concern was precious and clear. Is it still with you?"

This was a liberating moment, because it provided a coherent position, grounded in prayer and tested by the community, from which to ask how the current issues related to the original gift. It then allowed the Friend and her committee to consider, if the concern remained with her, whether she might not find another way to act upon it, or if it had changed, how so, and how did it relate to the current difficulties. Perhaps more important than any other effect, this return to the gift enabled the Friend and the others to reconnect with the moment of grace and power that had been felt, and from that place of health to consider whether the way forward was blocked, or the call was to persistence, or some new path was called for. Therefore, the key move was to remember that the Friend and her community had been given a gift, in the form of the concern, and they shared the burden of its right care.

This attitude must follow, if we believe in fact that concerns and leadings are the result of God at work in the heart. While you may be led down a lonely path, with no real company, and your meeting may not be led to take up the concern with you, yet it is a little, precious treasure, for whose welfare everyone should feel solicitous, like a spiritual guest that has come to visit for a while. Hospitality may primarily rest in one heart, but the whole community should be anxious to care for it.

22

On opportunities: part 1

One way that the Quaker spiritual system of earlier days offers us instruction for our own time lies in the place that worship, in many forms, was assumed to be part of daily life. In the insistence upon "frequent times of retirement" for prayer, Friends echo the experience of almost every religious practice of East or West. A distinctive note, however, is heard in the Quaker use of group worship. Aside from the gatherings on First Days, Friends of an earlier day made sure that the unpredictable presence of God played a central role in many aspects of pastoral care and religious instruction. They developed methods for attending to the divine dimension at home, at work, or in the interstices of the normal. The usual rhythms of life were perturbed, to further the inward work of Christ. Such incursions of worship have been called "opportunities."

The word "opportunity" implies a great deal about the dynamics of our spiritual life. These occasions are gifts, interruptions in the routine, that provide another, less institutional way to meet the living God, mediated by a living human messenger. If someone is led to offer an unscheduled occasion for worship in public or in the home, this is to be accepted gratefully, because you never can tell what God has in store. In years past, Friends assumed that, for example, Rebecca Jones's visiting with all the families in a meeting was as much a sign of God's care and activity as was Jonah's trip to Nineveh, that great city. The opportunity is an evidence of God at work, a stirring of the waters as at the pool of Siloam.

There are two kinds of events that Friends have called opportunities. The first is a wholly spontaneous thing, which many of us can report from our own experience: a group of Friends is talking, and in the midst of the conversation, someone feels overcome by a sense of awe or presence, and falls into silent worship. As the concerned Friend is seized by this sense of spiritual attentiveness, others become aware that something is happening, and the concern spreads among the group, which finds itself, to the wonder of all, worshipping deeply for a little time. The Friend who was at the epicenter of this event may speak out of the silence, or the group may gradually "surface" again, and continue its socializing as before—yet with some lingering effects of reverence and spiritual exercise.

The second kind of event that Friends have called an opportunity is different because it is more intentional, and it was at one time a principal means of pastoral care in our meetings. It has almost fallen out of use, partly because modern lives tend to have less space than lives once did, partly because the practice is very demanding. But as the concern for intervisitation and the renewal of ministry among unprogrammed Friends has proceeded, many Friends have been led into a renewal of this kind of opportunity as well. This is the focus of the present chapter.

This sort of opportunity can take place in the course of travel under concern, as a result of a special concern for one group or another, or just in the normal course of life in a meeting. Friends travelling in the ministry today tend to do so by invitation rather than under the pressure of their own concern, and the scheduled event can end up as the sole focus of the visit. Nevertheless, it is good when Friends look for the chance to meet with individuals or small groups in the course of other public tasks, and build some extra time into their schedules to allow for the possibility. Increasingly Friends travelling under concern will feel it right to stay in an area for more than a day or two, "visiting in depth," and opportunities can be a part of this.

The effectiveness of this kind of visitation from outside, however, depends on the extent to which we become familiar with other kinds of opportunities, when we feel specifically drawn to meet with a Friend or group of Friends within one's own meeting. It can be nourishing in any case; but if the community culture is familiar and comfortable with opportunities, it can encourage visitors to suggest them (when they might have been hesitant to otherwise). Therefore it is good when Friends can encourage each other to seek opportunities, and be very open to possible settings for them. The concern to request an opportunity can be of many different kinds. For example, one Friend in our meeting has sought opportunities in many meetings with Friends who tend to speak often in worship; other Friends have felt led to visit politicians in a worshipful manner; and sometimes in the context of worship, or a time of quiet contemplation, a face or name will appear to the worshiper with a sense that it would be good to meet with that person. This might be because he or she has something particular to say to that person. It is possible that you will feel led to seek an opportunity with someone because you yourself might gain guidance or counsel from that person, or perhaps for no reason that you can see. It may just feel important to take time to sit quietly in God's presence together.

Some may find themselves drawn to people in a particular station in life, such as shut-ins, or couples about to marry, or newcomers to the meeting, or frequent speakers in meeting. Other people over the years have become watchful for the Guide's promptings toward individuals, and can implement these occasional leadings in a gentle and acceptable manner. Such Friends have done a great deal of the pastoral care in meetings, in a way that is complementary to the work of the oversight committee or other "structural" devices. A special case of this is when a Friend feels called to visit systematically some or all of the membership. It is good to remember also that it was once common for meetings to appoint a small committee to undertake visits to every household in the meeting, and though these were sometimes undertaken with a desire to more strictly enforce the discipline, they were also often times of support, refreshment, and deeper acquaintance.

The opportunities that arise within the bounds of a meeting are especially important, but such occasions can be hard to undertake because we are timid about meeting so intimately, or because we feel embarrassed about being overtly religious, or for any number of reasons. When someone proposes such a visit with you, you may wonder if the initiator has some agenda, some criticism, or some work for you. It is important that the person seeking an opportunity be very clear that "love was the first motion," and that God's love and presence form the fundamental content of the visit, within and beyond any other transaction or content that may be included.

What happens in such an opportunity? One can generalize about this in the same way (and with the same limitations) that one can about meeting for worship. Here is a composite picture, assuming that two people are involved (though of course more might be).

Typically, after meeting at the agreed time and place, the two spend a little time connecting with each other in conversation. Before settling in, they should make any arrangements that will keep the time of worship relaxed and uninterrupted. It is helpful to be clear about any logistics or other details that may affect the session, and to make necessary arrangements before settling into worship. If there is some necessary limitation of time or otherwise, arrangements can be made then. If there is some specific topic that is part of the occasion, the two might address that if it is needed in preparation (as in a meeting for clearness).

The two then fall silent, and worship proceeds. The silence in such a situation can be of an extraordinary quality, and the intimacy of the setting, and of the agreement to meet together before God, make such times precious.

The worship can continue for a long time, though often the opportunity will be on the order of half an hour, more or less. It is hard to say, though, because the session may develop in such a way that deep worship may mix with conversation over a lengthy period.

Often, though not always, words will be spoken out of the silence; one or both may have a message on their hearts for the other. Vocal prayer often flows more freely in such a session than at other times, and can develop in extraordinary ways. In fact, the opportunity may be especially powerful as a "school of prayer."

The words that come may or may not be personal in their bearing. Many Friends can testify that they have been given tasks, warnings, prophecies, or specific encouragement in such sittings, when a gifted Friend "speaks to their condition;" but this is not to be expected nor forced, for when it is not from God, the counterfeit is obvious and can be harmful. The opportunity has been one of the principal settings in which ministers have received counsel, and "infant ministers" encouraged in their calling.

Very often, whether words are spoken or not, one feels especially searched, comforted, opened, and loved. Even if the session has no apparent results, the people involved feel they have been refreshed in spirit, and often in body as well.

The time of focused worship will come to an end as the Friends begin to move about or otherwise signal that this time of special attention is over. Now may come the sweetest fruits of the opportunity, as the two exchange thoughts or feelings that may have arisen in the silence. The concern that has led to the meeting may come out most fully here, liberated by the unity found in worship. The conversation will have a leisurely, tender quality, and the sense that both are listening keenly will remain, even when words replace deep silence.

Modern Friends have incorporated some of this experience in our meetings for clearness and in some other small group gatherings. Worship sharing groups and committees often have opportunities of the spontaneous kind, when their gathering is especially permeated with the sense of God's presence and action, and the relationships among the group members deepen in a tangible way. These occasions, welcome and valuable as they are, are not enough, however. If we are to take up sincerely the challenge to be constantly aware of the presence of God throughout the day, and in all settings, we need to help each other become more alert and responsive to that presence, and less self-conscious about doing so. It is very difficult to open our schedules and perhaps our homes to others for such an event, and at least as difficult to suggest it. Many have a circle of acquaintances with whom the idea is comfortable and almost expected as part of their social visits. This is a wonderful addition to these relationships, and a good way to cultivate experience with opportunities, but the chances we have to seek and acknowledge God's presence in all of life are not limited to such customary settings. This is another way in which we can keep alive the "experimental" nature of Quaker life.

23
On opportunities: part 2

The previous chapter provides, as it were, a general overview and introduction to the idea of the "opportunity." Here I wish to spend some time on the visitor's perspective.

I have found that the times when I have requested to worship with a family or an individual have been among the high points of my spiritual journey. These high points came when I arrived at the house very conscious of what a blessing it was simply to be welcomed there, and clear that my first purpose was to draw near to the light of Christ in each of the people present.

This inward clarity removed my anxiety, and allowed me to sit easily with the person(s) being visited. It also freed me in a surprising way from any preconceptions I had about the visit, or the person being visited. I was most grateful for this when I had some strong feeling, either positive or negative, towards the Friend, and I was enabled in simplicity and a real sweetness to see that person in some measure of gospel love, which in important ways is not personal, yet embraces the person before you.

I found this was true as well, when I had requested to sit with the person with a definite concern in mind. Even if, for example, I had come because this Friend had recently been much more active in some ministry, and it seemed like a good time to come and encourage or otherwise be present as she explored the new dimensions in her spiritual life and practice, I have found it very valuable to sit down and reach towards the light first, and not address the issue that I thought had brought me there. In this way, I was able to be a servant to the life in that person, as much as I had capacity for, and the session ended up being nourishing for us both.

It is good to remember that an opportunity may include more than one way of communication. One or both may

speak out of the silence in real ministry to the other, sometimes the words or the silence or both are just preambles to a
leisurely, friendly conversation in which the light is very much
felt to be present. Sometimes, the whole opportunity is a slow,
reflective conversation, with pauses in which the participants
reach towards the presence again, just checking in to make
sure that the next words said are authentic.

It is important in a session like this to be very wary of giving
advice, which can too often lead one to speak glibly. Advice
may be given, for sure, but it should really be drawn from the
moment, with much care. In times past, Friends visiting a
home might really "preach" at or to the person present, and
be tempted in a way to play at being a Quaker minister, rather
than rendering actual service. Counterfeit, even if self-delusion, is harmful. It is now rare that anyone requests an opportunity, and the visit you are making might be the only such
event that the visited Friend has ever had. If it is not done
humbly, sincerely, and courageously, the result may be to damage the faith of both of you. It may lessen respect for the idea
of opportunities, and the experience of prayer; and may also
lessen respect for you, the visitor. Our faith is weak enough, in
these days, that we should be very careful of damaging it with
anything fake. John William Graham wrote,

> I have once experienced this family sitting from an American
> Friend in my youth. I regret to say that it was all wrong in my
> case, and I thought it was pretence. The gift cannot be had by
> routine. (Graham 1933, 34)

In fact, in my experience, the deepest and sweetest times
have been those in which, if words are spoken during the
"waiting worship," they are prayer. I have remembered vividly
a time when a beloved minister visited my house, and we sat
together before bedtime, in worship. As was often true of him,
he was led to pray aloud for us, long and sweetly thanking
God for many things about my family. The power of the
prayer came because his thanks centered on an area which
was a place where much trouble was brewing, though I did
not know it, and so could not have spoken it. He never knew

how his prayer affected my life, but as he poured out simple, warm words of gratitude, my eyes were opened to see the unseen darkness; and so some healing began.

So, too, I have found in my own case, that when I have been most empty, and most centered on the Lord's presence with us, I have been led into prayer of a kind I had not otherwise experienced, and it was the gift that needed to be given. In this way, in such times of direct vulnerability of one person to another, one can see experimentally the wisdom of the Lord, and his mercy, at work in his children.

On the basis of this experience, therefore, I think it important to bring the following points to any Friend who feels drawn to make family or personal visits under concern:

- If you have a specific concern that you're travelling under, make sure you don't press it in the worship time, unless it returns with a real sense of life and appropriateness. If you feel a rebuke or resistance that is more than shyness, heed it! Your presence there in love is the fundamental gift, so stay with that if you are in doubt.

- Be willing to have the time pass quietly. As long as you stay with your Guide, the value of the visit will emerge. Most Friends are happy just to have worship in their homes, which often of itself is a real pleasure. In every journey in the ministry (however nearby), the fundamental message is the love of God at work among us.

- Make sure to start by being open, and holding each person present in prayer, being careful to be present with them, so that the meeting is centered on them and on their lives. If then you are led into words, be confident that as long as you remain in a tender place, the words may be few but appropriate.

- On the one hand, it is important not to fall into the trap of clairvoyant sham, on the other it is important to speak truth if one is really convinced it is true. If the message comes and persists with light, compassion, and power, it is likely to be safe. If it comes with the *appearance* of power [that is, with urgency], but not light and compassion, beware!

I would like to add something here about sitting with a Friend with whom you feel you must raise a difficult issue. I will speak personally here, but very carefully, and therefore a little in the abstract, out of respect for others involved.

I have a few times had to speak to Friends, who were also personal friends, in warning, because I had a very strong perception that the state of their personal lives was such that it rendered them temporarily unfit to serve in the ministry to which they felt called at that time. There was no way to express hesitation about their going on as usual, without addressing the specific issues which seemed an impediment. In these cases, my concern primarily was that their first responsibility was to deal with troubled relationships, and secondarily that if they went ahead as though nothing were wrong, their condition would be evident, and bring reproach on the whole idea of service under obedience to the Holy Spirit, rather than out of more personal motives. In one of these cases, I was so focused on the pain I thought I might cause, however cautiously I raised the issue, that I fear I was not able to speak in love as well as truth, and the bond of trust and friendship between us was damaged, a source of lasting pain for me.

In another case, some years later, I was somehow able to wait long enough to get a clear sense of the Friend's gift, which had been validated by Friends before, and exercised helpfully across our yearly meeting. Waiting until I could feel God present, and then sympathize with the troubled Friend, sharing the friend's regret that a real, living concern had to be set aside for a while until the Friend was clear again, I was given words which spoke to the witness in that person. Thanks to that, the words I spoke were heard as the reproof that they were, but also as a message of encouragement to move through to a new freedom.

There are few services more rewarding than visiting in homes, or with families, or individuals. It has been the school in which I have learned most intensively how it feels to rely upon God's guidance rather than my own judgment, and worked hardest to reach the place of simple and truthful reliance. It is for this reason that there are few things more costly to the minister who is faithful, even if you go away rewarded with a sense of joy and assurance that all was well: the cost and the joy are both true aspects of the experience. It is humbling, staggering, to read descriptions of Rebecca Jones or Elias Hicks visiting seventy families in a week! Yet it is encouraging, too. I do not need to emulate these people in anything except willingness to serve, but their example makes me ask, am I doing all that I really should be doing? Lord, is there anything more?

Note on "public" meetings for worship as opportunities

There are stirrings amongst many these days to open Quaker worship more widely, and to be more inventive about holding "public meetings" outside the safe walls of the meetinghouse. Silent, worshipful vigils are common as part of our witness for peace and justice. Some meetings have arranged "open house" events, actively extending invitations to Quaker worship, and sometimes providing a little quiet instruction about what we find valuable about our silent worship, and what we do during it. Often an important motivation for such events is to open the door to those who might find Quakerism valuable, if only they knew a little about it.

Beyond these valuable activities, however, I believe more is required of us. We are also called, I feel, to invite others to share Christ directly, not primarily in order to introduce them to Quakerism and bring them into our meetings, but to encourage them to turn to the light and follow it. This is different from "telling about," and "explaining."

This is scary and feels almost unnatural to Friends, who are otherwise quite bold in advocating for their concerns. It does challenge us to examine the nature of what we have found about God: with all our seeking, what have we found? I believe that experience with the opportunity, as described above, is a productive pathway forward. In a very few cases, I have been in such opportunities with non-Friends, who knew nothing about Quakerism. God was present, and guided us into prayer and sharing that was profound, moving, and quite unselfconscious.

This, it seems to me, is how "appointed meetings" should be seen: as opportunities, with a few or with many, in which the minister's role is to seek after the divine life in those present, and rely on the inward teacher to reach those present, and bring forth the words or worship that might be needed then. Framing the challenge in this way helps me bear in mind the sweetness, trust, and boldness that such an event requires, and helps me see also the spiritual, intellectual, and emotional work it demands, to explicitly preach the Gospel as Friends understand it.

24

On intervisitation

Many have written on one or another aspect of intervisitation. I do not intend to write a complete treatise here,[15] nor will I rehearse the reasons that a widespread renewal of mindful visitation is necessary to the survival and faithfulness of Friends witness. I only wish to advise you to seek the root of the action in love, to encourage plainness and patience in the concern, and to encourage you to seek to be free of current convention.

The root of the action

First, as to the root of the action. You may or may not have a particular concern in mind when you go out to visit a meeting or meetings. Yet as with any specific enactment of a sense of concern for the ministry, I think that your work will have the greatest good effect if you wait to find whether and where the springs of love and divine life connect with this opening before you appear in the work.

This is even true when you have had an invitation to come and speak on a topic to a workshop or some other forum. It is wise to be suspicious of what is very easy, draws on your practiced strengths and accomplishments, and can be treated as an everyday transaction. For example, you may have been asked to come and offer information or reflections on a very specific topic, such as the meeting for worship, or the peace testimony, or some aspect of our discipline, or some political or social question—whatever you may have a useful knowledge of. Take the time to explore how this invitation relates to your basic concern for the abundance of life in the people of God, and more specific concerns you may be carrying in your

---

[15] See, for example, Samuel Bownas, *Description of the Qualifications necessary to a Gospel Minister* (1989), and the very recent Abbott and Parsons, *Walk Worthy of Your Calling* (2004).

ministry. You may well find, upon waiting with this question, that your right course is to offer what you have been asked to; no doubt this will typically be the case.

Yet the waiting and asking beforehand may transform your understanding of the experience, even while you offer the fruits of your experience or learning that led to the invitation in the first place. It may not even change the words you choose when making your presentation. The effect may be only to sharpen your awareness that in such an event, people's spirits are engaged and active, and therefore fresh openings may come unexpectedly to those who are on the alert; or fears and confusions may arise, whose consequences reach beyond the content or the intent of the specific occasion. You may only be given the chance to hold the tendered soul in prayer; or some other opportunity may arise. In any case, your centering your service in the life, and a real feeling of care for those you meet, makes it more likely that the occasion will facilitate a spiritual encounter, along with the intellectual and social transactions that take place. When you are called to such an event, however typical a workshop or forum it may be, your calling means that you need to be on watch!

Plainness

Second, as to plainness, or directness. I have known ministers whose concern for intervisitation has centered first and foremost on presence, on just coming because of the love they feel for those visited. Rufus Jones famously said that the travelling ministry in the eighteenth and nineteenth century was like the blood circulating within the body of Friends, connecting all parts to each other, and carrying nourishment to every extremity. Very often, these travelling Friends had their greatest effect just in arriving from their home meeting, demonstrating that they were in fellowship with the visited. The simple fact of their presence, out of a sense of kinship in the Spirit, was a powerful testimony to the reality of God's activity in their lives. If they were led to provide teaching, prayer, exhortation, advice—that was an additional blessing, for sure, and to be hoped for. I believe, however, that Friends are deeply famished for lack of the former, simple gift of presence in love.

Therefore, please consider whether, when no specific task lies on you, you are not drawn simply in gospel love to be near other Friends, either in their homes, or in a meeting nearby or distant. I have found that if I have made such a visit, just out of a sense of love, and not said a word in the line of ministry, but after meeting have introduced myself and said that I came out of concern or love, just that gift alone had a tendering effect. After all, the aim of all our work is more abundant life and an increase in the sense of fellowship, and of the presence of the Lord. If you enable Friends to feel those, you have done them a great service, though you said no word.

William Taber, in describing his work as a released Friend for Ohio Yearly Meeting, gives a very effective description of this simple response of love, in this case for his yearly meeting:

> As I began to take up the concern . . . I was given the vision that my most important task was to draw near to the light of Christ in each of our meetings and in every individual; and to ask others to share in awareness of this light. . . . Therefore, I first visited members here and there, asking them to join me in a continuing work of prayer, recognizing this light and praying for its growth in our midst, even while we were travelling or working. For several years, then, I saw my most important task to be to allow myself to be drawn to individuals or groups, so that we might enter into awesome fellowship where two or three are gathered in His Name, and the light grows. In my mind's eye, each meeting seemed like a cluster of light, and its members were points of light; and I was required to circulate among these points of light, so that our silent recognition of the light, our sharing on this level of consciousness, would allow this light to grow. (Taber 1985, 229–30)

Even a concern that has a specific "content," such as a peace or social justice theme, or a desire to encourage Friends' prayer practices, should first and foremost be rooted in love. No one has expressed that with more power than John Woolman, writing about his concern for the Lenni-Lenappe and Susquehanah Indians, when he identifies love as the first motion; "and *then* a concern arose to visit among the Indians" [my emphasis].

Freedom from convention

Finally, about sticking to conventions, a theme to which we must return constantly. Most of the time these days, travel in the ministry takes the form of a gifted Friend being invited to a meeting (monthly, quarterly, or yearly) to give a talk or workshop. With appropriate discernment and prayer, this can be a valuable kind of ministry—but it has too much become the typical, that is the paradigm, kind of event. My yearly meeting, New England, has established an intervisitation program which helps make meetings aware of Friends who are willing to come and visit with a particular concern. Other yearly meetings and Friends organizations have similar committees. This is very useful, both to the meetings, and to the Friends, since it is a way of encouraging Friends in a concern, and stimulating circulation among the meetings. It also stimulates our awareness of meetings in particular need of visitors, because of isolation, or some issue exercising the meeting. Yet we still need something in addition to this very organization-centered sort of activity.

This useful system has not led to a renaissance of travel in the ministry of the old style, in which the minister feels a prophetic call to draw near to the life of God somewhere, with or without a specific message. This is too precious an element of our religious life to let die. When a Friend comes under obedience to God, this is an opportunity for an unexpected blessing for the visited meeting, for individual Friends, and the visitor. Neither the visitor nor the visited can predict, if they are really open, what might occur; and if they accept the opportunity with thanks, the spiritual nourishment may be very great. Even if no signal event seems to occur, it is valuable to remember that God may visit us at any time, inwardly or in the person of another, and we may entertain angels unawares (Heb. 13:2). Thus we grow in the precious gifts of gratitude and simplicity.

Therefore, Friend, if you are visiting to do a task at a meeting, for example, to lead a workshop or give a talk, be alert to the possibility that you have an opening to do something more. This might take the form of staying longer in a home, requesting a meeting for worship, visiting particular Friends who are in need, or whose concern you wish to encourage, or whom you wish to thank for something they have done for you. In addition to the specific preparations you may need to make for the workshop or address you have been invited for, make sure to spend time in prayer, with the question on your mind: Is there anything else, Lord?

Many meetings exhort their members to travel to other meetings. Most Friends don't do it, though. It is even rarer for Friends to undertake systematic intervisitation under concern, and part of that may well be owing to a misapprehension of what forms intervisitation "ought" to take. From what precedes, I hope the reader feels freed from the notion that one cannot travel unless one has a "message" to deliver, some specific issue to bring to meetings.

Now let us just consider how the service may take shape, in logistical terms. I have four specific issues in mind: first, finding the right timescale for the concern; second, keeping the travel rooted in the home meeting; third, being open to leadings for unusual messages, for example, to specific individuals or groups; fourth, travel with a companion.

Time

First, it need not be conducted in an extended block of time. That is, a real concern to travel may not require you to set aside weeks or months of uninterrupted focus on the concern. There are many accounts from the heyday of the travelling ministry that tell how ministers under a particular concern wove it into the fabric of the rest of their lives, dedicating evenings or Sunday afternoons to the work. Even so great a traveller as Elias Hicks often carried out concerns for family visitation or for visits to Friends schools by a series of separate meetings over the course of weeks or months, interleaved with his occupation with "temporal concerns around home."

This has been the most common pattern for my own meeting visits. For example, in 2003 I felt a strong leading to visit meetings in New England. I brought the concern to my monthly meeting. In the resulting discernment I was asked to set aside one Sunday a month for the concern, since our meeting is small, and every member's absence is significant. As I followed that discipline, I still felt that more was needed. After waiting with this disquiet for a while, I found ways to visit during the week with meetings on ministry and counsel. In this way I learned more about each meeting, and also could visit more deeply with a few Friends than I might have done only coming to First Day meetings.

Yet when it happens that one is able to concentrate only on a trip for intervisitation, there are special gifts that can come from the intensity and unbroken focus, especially if one has companions with whom one can sometimes speak frankly and freely in reflecting on the experience. Here again, the use of a notebook or journal can be invaluable both for reflection at the time and also for use later as an aide-mémoir.

Relation with the meeting

Second, while the intervisitation comes from a concern that has arisen for you, it is also an outgrowth of the meeting's life. This is true even when there is some resistance or discomfort about the concern, or about the whole process of travel in the ministry. Therefore, it is an important discipline, for which you will come to be grateful very soon, to have in the forefront of your mind that you come with the loving greetings of your Friends for the meeting or people visited. It is also important to be aware of the need to report back to the meeting when the concern is completed (or, if it extends over a long period of time, at points during the service). Your experience of other meetings and their conditions, interests, challenges, and activities can provide valuable nourishment for Friends at home. Your reporting, as well, is a way for the meeting to feel the rightness of your concern (and their support of it) in one more way, and to get some understanding of your own growth as a result of the service. It is a common experience of many Friends with concerns (for peace, prison work, etc.) that they have trouble connecting this point of excitement and inspiration in their lives with the life of their meeting, and that their meeting doesn't quite know how to include their efforts. Travel under concern, which requires a minute from the meeting, and thereby leaves open the expectation of a report at the end, is one valuable way in which meetings can gain some experience with this question, and learn to expect reports on concerns. Thus, when meetings find a way to support a concern for gospel ministry (for which our tradition has much guidance to offer), they may also find that the lessons learned encourage them to find appropriate ways to encourage other kinds of gifts and callings.

Others have written effectively about the process of clearness and pastoral care for Friends who have a concern to travel. In this connection, I wish only to add that sometimes these clearnesses do not go deep enough in exploring how the concern is actually rooted in the life of the minister. It is not uncommon to feel a clear, strong leading to travel, but not yet be mature enough to carry the concern appropriately. The integrity of the message depends upon the evidence of the Spirit at work, but the power and meaning of it are given credibility and force by the minister's integrity in other ways. John Griffith tells of a time when Friends explored beyond the concern itself, to examine if his preparation for it included ordering his life to follow the leading faithfully:

> A certificate was prepared, setting forth their unity with my service in the ministry, and with my intended journey; desiring my labouring therein might tend to the edification of the churches where my lot should be cast, and for my return to them again in peace; also expressing that I had settled my outward affairs to the satisfaction of that meeting—for I had acquainted friends how I had settled them, as I thought it concerned them to be satisfied in that, as well as other things; it being my earnest desire

to have the full concurrence of my brethren in so great an undertaking. (Griffith 1779, 67)

Speaking to conditions

Third, forms of "speaking to conditions." The journals and Quaker folklore are replete with examples of Friends speaking very directly to the condition of specific Friends or meetings. This is to be expected sometimes, if part of the service of the ministry is to help people see where they are, and what the state of their spiritual life is. A famous example is the time when Anne Wilson, visiting a meeting, speaks directly to the young black-smith's apprentice, Samuel Bownas, who sits in the rear of the meetinghouse drowsing in the quiet. As he wrote in his journal,

> [O]ne First Day, being at meeting, a young woman named Anne Wilson was there and preached. She was very zealous, and I fix-ing my eye upon her, she, . . . pointed her finger at me, uttering these words with much power: "A traditional Quaker, thou comest to meeting as thou went from it the last time, and goest from it as thou came to it, but art no better for thy coming; what wilt thou do in the end?" This was so suited to my condition that . . . I was smitten to the ground, but, turning my thoughts inward, in secret I cried, Lord, what shall I do to help it? (Bownas 1839, 3)

Many journal writers describe moments in their travels when they had "close work," and felt led to speak in very pointed terms about the state of the meeting, or the leader-ship, or the appearance of the young people. In that culture rough-tongued elders, speaking "plain," could say, "Friend, thy words have not the savor of truth!"[16] This has long been unknown among us, and the idea of its returning is disturbing to imagine. On one hand, it is so easy to feel judgmental, to assume the cloak of "prophet," scorning to speak "smooth things," and enjoying the pleasures of self-righteousness. It is likely to be quite rare that one is securely enough situated in

---

[16] Job Scott in his journal speaks eloquently of how harsh rebuke can be harmful and counterproductive, and masquerades as "plain speaking" when it may really have baser roots. See the anecdote from Edward Hicks's journal, in chapter 17 "On being dipped into sympathy."

the Spirit as to speak such a message in a way that it reaches to the seed, and is not merely a personal exercise. On the other hand, such speaking to conditions is a very great risk for the speaker. There are so many ways that we may be mistaken, that such directness is frightening. It is easier, perhaps, for us to "speak truth to power," to confront a politician whose policies we oppose, than to confront deplorable conditions amongst our Friends. We prefer to speak in generalities, hoping that if the shoe fits the right person will try it on; this is less confrontational than Anne Wilson was. Perhaps we are not brave enough to accept when we have been given a very direct message for a specific person or group. Greater experience in "opportunities" and prayer with one or two others can provide some tutelage in this regard, perhaps.

Yet while I believe that we should be more open to this kind of specific speaking, I do not believe that if we are faithful it will usually take the form of warning or denunciation. The impulse for this kind of message very often comes out of personal emotion—anger, fear, frustration, or the desire to enhance one's position. If a direct challenge is to come sometimes, I believe that it will most often take a form that may speak of shortcomings, but mostly speak of invitation to the love of God, and in that spirit reach to God's inward witness: "It takes its kingdom by entreaty, and not with contention, and keeps it by lowliness of mind."

I would like to recount a case from my own experience. In one year, I twice visited a meeting in New England, one which I know fairly well and am very fond of. In this meeting it is the custom for children to sit in meeting while it gathers, and then, after about 15 minutes, to go out for First Day School. On both occasions that year, I felt strongly compelled to stand and speak before the children went out. The messages that I was given were decidedly not "for the children," though in one of them, I was led to speak to the children, pointing out how the message related to them as well as to their elders. At the rise of meeting, when introductions went around, I felt again a sense of requirement. This time, I felt led to explain to the meeting that I had twice been led to offer messages earlier than was customary so that the children were present. The sense of urgency and concern made me ask: Was there a message beyond the words of the message? It seemed that they might well ask themselves what their children's experience of worship was: was it always in the controlled, "introductory" mode, or did they have the opportunity to experience a full meeting for worship, even if the silence and the ministry might seem "over their heads?" I felt urgently that this good and wholesome meeting was being called to try a new thing.

I was very worried that this might sound like "giving the meeting advice," which would have felt presumptuous. Yet I was very conscious also of a real sense of God's love present among us, and felt "used" by the Spirit, and accompanied by it in my speaking. The meeting received my words with no sense of defensiveness, but rather welcomed them, and several spoke to me afterwards of how my message felt both striking and loving. Once again, I believe the key ingredient here was the real sense of love, and the impulse to offer more abundant life—therefore, there was a positive invitation, which carried with it a probing question, rather than an accusation of short-coming, followed by a prescription.

Travel companions

Fourth, travel with a companion. In the "classical" model of travel in the ministry, the minister should travel with an approved companion. This has deep roots, not only in Quaker practice, but also in New Testament models of the apostles travelling in pairs for mutual support. The practice is very valuable on many fronts. Before some reflections on this, however, a note of caution.

I think it is important not to take "travel in pairs" as a hard and fast rule. Very many occasions are recorded in the journals and other narratives from times past, in which a rightly concerned minister travels alone. This has often been my experience as well, especially when the service takes the form of several separate episodes. Sometimes it is possible to find someone to travel with, but sometimes it is not, and if the service is pressing, you must get on with it. When this is the case, it is useful for you, the traveller, to take care beforehand to recall that you must be in a listening frame of mind, and go ready to learn, as well as speak—and as ready to be silent as to speak. In addition, it may be that when you arrive, a particular Friend there appears as a counsellor and guide for you, though no preparation was made ahead of time. If you feel you need it, a request for prayer often brings a warm and ready response.

Much of my own travel has been to meetings or individuals within my yearly meeting, and I have interwoven the visiting with my working schedule and family life. For this reason, it has most often been the case that I have gone alone. It has been very educative to spend the time en route in prayer, in part getting free of preconceptions, and in part looking forward with a kind of eager attention to learning and listening as sensitively as possible in the meeting I am approaching. The time alone has been helpful, therefore, in my own training and discipline, and I believe that it has meant that I am more "present" to the meeting than I might have been if I were accompanied. In a sense, the encounter is more direct. In many such cases, I have found someone at the visited meeting who has provided the kind of grounding that a travelling companion can. I have learned better to recognize when I am not as centered as I'd like to be: to expect some wishful thinking or self-delusion, and to relax in God's presence to let the illusion fade away.

Briefly, here, we can touch upon the great help that the companion can render in helping to make logistical arrangements to support a minister's work—notifying people ahead of time, overseeing travel arrangements, writing down phone numbers and names, etc.—the sort of work of which Job Scott wrote, in the 1790s, that "it is of more importance than many realize."

In addition, your companion can provide important support in prayer, before, during, and after a visit, and also be a trusted confidante. In addition, if the travel is for any length of time, having a familiar face can be a great solace. To refer to Job Scott's letters again, he notes, after tenderly empathizing with his wife left behind while he is on a visit to the southern states, that at least she is surrounded by their home and friends. Meanwhile he arrives day after day at a community, connects with the Friends there, joins them for worship and perhaps conversation, and then has to pull up roots and do it all over again with a new set of strangers—a wearisome experience, however welcoming the Friends are.

It is common these days to speak of the person under concern as "the minister," and the companion as "the elder," but I would like to point out that this should be taken primarily as a description of functions that each may perform on the trip, both in acting on leadings during the time, and in supporting each other along the way. Ministers travelling together can develop deep bonds and provide deep comfort and frank commentary to each other, and Quaker history is full of such teams that become as close as brothers or sisters.

Samuel Bownas's journal describes many occasions, especially during his younger years, in which he and other young ministers travelling together encouraged each other as they went along:

> We took meetings in our way, as they suited, and I found my companion under a great concern to speak something in meetings, but very backward and loath to give up to it. I gave him what encouragement I could; and in Tewksbury meeting after some struggle in himself, he stood up, and appeared very much to his own, and Friends' comfort, and so in every meeting after, till we came to Bristol; and indeed he appeared more like an elder in the work than a babe. At Bristol he did not get through what he had before him to his liking, and sat down under great discouragement; but I cheered him up as well as I could, by giving him an account of my experiences; and when we came to the little country meetings again, he did finely, and gathered strength and experience in the work. (Bownas 1839, 40)

The most satisfying experience I have had with such teamwork was on a two-week trip to Cuba, in which I accompanied a Friend who had a concern to visit the meetings there. His was the concern, and at every meeting I worked to make sure that he had an opportunity to share. Yet I also felt free to act on openings for service that came to me, and he supported me just as freely. In fact, at that time I had had more experience in travel in the ministry than he, and so in some ways it felt that my feeling free to act as led would help him do the same; and so it turned out. In preparing for the trip, we discussed how we would work together—on what points each of us especially wanted feedback (or reassurance), questions each of us was carrying about our visit, and also reasons that each of us found in the other for confidence. During the trip, we both offered informal and spontaneous comments to each other, and took the time occasionally for more formal conversations: How has it gone with you recently? What have you noticed? Is there anything particular you think should happen next? The visit to Cuba went well, and as far as we know was acceptable to the Friends visited. The collaboration between us was very sweet, and both of us learned much from each other, as well as the very basic lesson in every place we went, which is that God is to be relied upon, as he opens human hearts to each other.

I end here with a quotation from Stephen Crisp, which leads from the present topic to the last chapter:

> And I was exercised, according to my ability, in visiting the assemblies of the Lord's people in Essex and Suffolk, where it lay upon me; and in helping and assisting the Lord's people according to my ability, both in their spiritual and temporal concerns, as the Lord God of my life gave me an understanding: for I gave up the ordering of my spirit unto Him; and he opened me in many things relating to the affairs of this world, that I might be as a staff to the weak in these things, and might stand by the widow and fatherless, and plead the right of the poor. In all which, I sought neither honor nor profit, but did all things freely, as I received of God: and he whom I served was my reward, so that I lacked nothing. Therefore, who would not praise the Lord, and who would not trust in His Name? (Crisp 1850, 151)

25

On taking joy in the service

These things have I spoken unto you, that my joy might remain
in you, and that your joy may be complete. (JOHN 15:11)

Jesus teaches us to expect joy in following him, and in our
unity through his Spirit with our brothers and sisters. Take
time to experience joy in the call to service, and in times when
you have served faithfully. The gospel ministry is costly; yet if it
is a concern you are carrying rightly, it is a path of rejoicing,
and growing peace. The increase of joy, and of confidence in
God's reliable presence, has always been accepted as evidence
that the minister has been faithful.

This is not to be mistaken for self-congratulation or a sense
of superiority, which are antithetical to the joy of which Jesus
spoke. In the inward training that we go through, we come
more and more to know how to anchor our life and service in
divine love, and find our fears diminished and defeated. We
become more sensitive to evil in ourselves, our society, and
those we meet. We become more compassionate, knowing the
many ways that we are likely to be mistaken, deluded, or limited by our personalities, our understandings, our experience,
our culture. We feel it more keenly when we come to recognize the seed's oppression, and we come to understand
Nayler's words, when he said that the spirit he felt "is con-
ceived in sorrow, and brought forth without any to pity it, nor
doth it murmur at grief and oppression . . . with the world's
joy it is murthered. I have fellowship therein with them who
lived in dens and desolate places in the earth."

Yet even so, we are given along with this a heightened sense
of gratitude. We become great in thanksgiving, and feel how
gratitude is a taproot of prayer and upwelling life. With Fox
we "rejoice to see the springs of life break forth in any," and
are free to take delight in the multitudinous evidences of the
life and light, in other people, in the natural world, even in

ourselves. As Lewis Benson wrote, "It is a wonderful thing to be called to the ministry of the Gospel of Jesus Christ." (Benson 1979, 51)

In being open to this service, and following it with increasing faithfulness and abandon, we are shaped and reshaped, sifted and refined, so that less and less stands between us and our sense of God's presence, in ourselves and in others. Ecstatic phrases cannot really convey the comfort, peace, delight, and safety that we feel in God's presence, and if our lives are more and more given to the service of this life in all, in waiting, in doing, in speaking, and in silence, then we are more and more surrounded by all these things, which can be summarized in the short powerful words: light, life, love.

APPENDIX 1

On being a recorded minister[17]

Some meetings still follow the practice of minuting or otherwise naming Friends whom they judge to have received a sustained gift in the ministry. Other meetings, where it has been disused for a long time or is unknown, debate whether this practice, or something like it, should be taken up again. From time to time I have been asked about my thoughts on the subject, as I am a person who has been so "recorded."

I think that this is a valuable conversation to have, as long as it explores the function which the institution arose to fill. I do not argue that where the institution has fallen out of use it should necessarily be recreated. I would like to claim the following, though:

First, that the institution is often misinterpreted, and this makes it harder to understand its possible relevance for today.

Second, that the institution served several purposes which Friends still need to accomplish. In this respect, therefore, it poses a challenge to Friends to find alternative structures if this one is no longer serviceable.

Third, I believe that this challenge is related to central questions of theology and practice among us about which it would be well to work towards a shared understanding.

In the course of the revision of our New England Yearly Meeting Discipline in 1985, and in other contexts, I have sat in on several weighty considerations of this topic, and although they have been good discussions, there has only been a slow progress of insight, and strong feelings "for" and "against" remain. This is a sign to me that we are not yet asking the right questions. It seems to me that the right questions have to do with the way our community recognizes (in the

[17] An update and revision of a presentation made at Pendle Hill in 1996. Certain passages redundant with earlier pages in this book were removed, but others retained for continuity of thought.

sense of "comes to see") the gifts being poured out upon us, *and* takes an appropriate, active role in their cultivation, without which the gifts will not bear fruit as they should.

All discussion about "machinery," or more politely "church polity," has to take second place to a focus on this central question. We are in a weakened condition, as a people, in part because of our lack of practical attention to the nurture of gifts. Talk about the recorded ministry only has value if it furthers our understanding of the tasks lying before us. How can we grow stronger as a witnessing, prophetic community? There are words we are not saying, deeds we are not doing, questions we are not asking, and I suspect that some of our weakness is related to the way we care for the gifts bestowed on our community. Furthermore, I believe that we are weaker than we might be, because the specific gifts of gospel ministry are not supported and nurtured as they could be.

I will sketch the basics of the history and procedures of recording, then a bit about my own experience of it. Finally, I will try to address its relevance to the larger question of nurturing gifts in the present day.

I should say that I will not speak about Friends' pastors here. The recording of ministers is a much older practice, by more than a century, than the calling of pastors by Friends meetings, and it is quite possible to discuss recording without reference to pastors at all. Though some have seen a clear continuity between the old practice, as known (say) in Woolman's time and the pastorate as it has developed in the past century or so, I believe that they are not the same thing, and are enactments of very different theologies. I also will not address anything about the variations in the practice of recording from one yearly meeting to another, though that might be interesting as well.

Finally, it is notable (and, I believe significant) that in most discussions about ministry, we end up focusing on vocal ministry, the ministry of the word. In part, this is because the gospel ministers, whose gift was the gift of articulation, felt it part of their duty to record their experiences as they sought to exercise their gift faithfully. This means that, from some periods of Quaker history, we have a lot of information about the growth, nurture, and pitfalls of gifts in vocal ministry. This does point up the central role that the ministry has played among us during the entire lifetime of the Quaker movement. On the other hand, some Friends, with other undoubted gifts, have not left us any such record of their life-cycle in ministry. Since Friends have not yet redressed this balance, we often find ourselves referring to the great body of history about vocal ministers, as a point from which to draw speculations or analogies about other kinds of ministers. I wish we could find a way to get around this artifact of our history! Nevertheless, the record of these ministers holds important instruction for anyone under a spiritual concern, and is a treasury that we have not profited from enough.

Some history

From the earliest days of the Quaker movement, Friends have assumed that, while anyone may be called to speak in meeting on a particular occasion, some seem to be called, appropriately and faithfully, to more responsibility or concern for the work than others. The assumption is that Christ is the head of the church, and pours out the gifts that the community needs. These gifts (tasks, responsibilities, abilities) come for longer or shorter periods of time, and vary in many other characteristics as well. Robert Barclay's articulation of this in his *Apology* is retained in some books of *Faith and Practice*:

> We do believe and affirm that some are more particularly called to do the work of the ministry, and therefore are fitted by the Lord for that purpose; whose work is more constantly and particularly to instruct, exhort, admonish, oversee, and watch over their brethren; and that . . . there is something more incumbent upon them in that respect than upon every common believer. (Barclay 2002 [1678], 274)

In the early days of the movement, Friends who felt the call to public ministry were in touch with each other by frequent meetings and in correspondence on a local, regional, and national level. They came forth spontaneously, and were intensely aware of the colleagueship, their special kinship with other public Friends, as a result of their shared calling.

By the 1670s, there was a regular meeting in London of all Public Friends who happened to be in town. They met for mutual support, and to work out who would go to which meetings in the coming week, so that "ministers should not go about in heaps." There was also discussion of places that might need special attention or support. Since this meeting was held on Second Day, it was always called the Second-Day Morning Meeting (or Morning Meeting, for short) and it continued until the early part of the twentieth century. (It also came to serve as a way-station for Friends correspondence, and as the censor of Friends publications in the yearly meeting, though it had no official status as part of the yearly meeting—it was not the same as the yearly meeting of ministers and elders, for example.)

The way you were accepted as a member of the Second-Day Morning Meeting was to sign in a big book on Second Day morning, as you came to attend. It happened in 1734 that a Friend signed in, who (other Friends thought) was not in unity with Friends, and his right to attend the meeting was challenged. After lengthy wrangling, the yearly meeting ruled that the Second-Day Morning Meeting could not exclude anyone who came with a letter from his monthly meeting attesting to the fact that this Friend was a minister in good standing there.

From these haphazard beginnings, there developed the following procedure, varying only slightly from place to place in Quakerdom for two centuries. In New England Yearly Meeting, this old procedure is intact, if rarely used. It goes like this: If a Friend gives evidence of a "sustained gift in the gospel ministry," then the local meeting on ministry and counsel brings it to the monthly meeting. If the meeting unites in this perception of the Friend, the matter is referred to the quarterly meeting on ministry and counsel, who appoints a committee to meet with the Friend in question, and the monthly meeting as well, if necessary. If the committee agrees with the monthly meeting, it makes a recommendation to the quarterly meeting on ministry and counsel, which if it concurs then passes the matter with a recommendation to the full quarterly meeting. If the quarterly meeting approves, it then informs the monthly meeting, and there is an end to it. In the old days, the only event that would mark the final approval (beyond the minute itself) is that the Friend would for the first time take his or her place on the facing benches at meeting. The recorded Friend would also become a member of the system of parallel meetings of ministers and elders, at the levels of monthly, quarterly, and yearly meetings. There was not a closed membership to the meeting of ministers and elders. There might well be more than one minister in a meeting (better if there was), or none. The meeting of ministers and elders (later often renamed the meeting or committee for ministry and oversight, ministry and worship, ministry and counsel, etc.) typically comprised the weightiest members of the meeting, and sometimes exerted a deadening effect on the meeting, as many contemporary accounts relate.

What was supposed to follow, after the minute was taken acknowledging the meeting's judgment that a gift had been given? "All" that was required of ministers was that they devote time to prayer and scriptural study, shaping their life to service, and then to do anything they were called by God to do, subject to the discernment of the meeting, and especially the elders of the meeting. They were to seek the society and counsel of more experienced ministers, though never to emulate them. They also were to be faithful in attendance at meetings for worship and business, and at meetings of ministry and counsel (monthly, quarterly, and yearly).

Friends ministers were never paid for their work, though if they could not bear the cost of something the meeting had agreed they were called to do, Friends were obliged to help, either with travel expenses or help at home while the minister was away. This was often done, judging from the evidence of journals and correspondence; but I know of no study of the practice.

London Yearly Meeting did away with the practice of recording ministers in 1924, while adopting advice to itself and its constituent meetings that Friends' gifts in the ministry, and the vigorous life of the spirit out of which all ministry springs, should be carefully nurtured. A retrospective address by T. H. Harvey in the 1940s suggested that the yearly meeting had not succeeded in its plan to care for the ministry by more "democratic" means. Nevertheless, the practice was dropped in most unprogrammed yearly meetings, either explicitly or through disuse, except in the Conservative ones, and in the united yearly meetings, such as Baltimore, New England, and New York. The practice also survived in some monthly meetings in Philadelphia Yearly Meeting and a few other places.

How has it looked for me, as one of the current crop of recorded ministers?

New England Yearly Meeting retained the practice of recording as part of its discipline. Two of the bodies which reunited in 1945 actively recorded gifts (though based on very different theologies of the ministry): the larger, pastoral yearly meeting and the smaller Wilburite group. I was recorded by Salem Quarterly Meeting at the request of Lynn Monthly Meeting in October 1983. I was serving as director of the Friends Home at the time and trying to revive the monthly meeting in Lynn, formerly a programmed meeting, but at that time unprogrammed. The meeting was dying, in fact it was laid down three years later, alas, after more than 300 years. I was 30 years old at the time of recording.

The whole process was something of interest, not to say curiosity, within the quarter, since it had been some many years since the quarterly meeting had recorded a minister, though ministers had transferred their recording with their membership, into the quarterly meeting from elsewhere. In addition, there were a couple of meetings within the quarter that had minuted their opposition to the practice of recording. They felt it was outmoded, and perhaps not in keeping with Friends principles, and no longer needed. During the 1950s, Henry Cadbury had provided some background discussion for Friends Meeting at Cambridge, as they considered the question, perhaps in the context of the revision of the discipline. He focused primarily on the question of recording as a way of fostering leadership within the meeting, and his own sense was that the meeting's present practices sufficed.

A further political complication is New England's status as a once-divided, now united yearly meeting—though the traces of the division, you might say the seams, are still visible, and only slowly being eradicated by the passage of time. As a result of this history there are several pastoral meetings in New England. Many Friends in unprogrammed meetings associate the practice of recording ministers with the pastoral system, with which they are uncomfortable. In fact, of the approximately 30 recorded ministers in New England Yearly Meeting at the time, the large majority were given that status in conjunction with some pastoral service, either within New England or elsewhere.

There were, therefore, a wide variety of views, both approving and disapproving of the action, and Friends were forthright in bringing both kinds of opinion to me. I had some interesting conversations with some people, who had a problem with the recording process, and with my being recorded. There was certainly an implication on the part of some that I was trying to make something happen, creating an authoritative status for myself, or committing some other sin of pride. A couple of elder Friends chided me, having made it clear that they didn't think that anyone "deserved" the status, since, for example, some ministers from the past had transgressed Friends principles unchastised, and many another Friend passed important, sanctified lives of service within and outside the Society and never had such a label.

Some who did not speak to me in a critical vein still wondered if I were casting in my lot with the "pastoral wing." This took place during a time when Christian language was emerging from the shadows in many meetings, and sometimes causing division. On the other hand some of the pastoral meetings in the yearly meeting were asserting some of their own needs and concerns, as opposed to those of the unprogrammed majority. It was an exciting time in New England, which is generally an exciting yearly meeting anyway. To be proposed as a Recorded Minister was to draw in a humble measure a lot of different kinds of lightning. This has continued, as conversations within meetings about supporting and recognizing gifts have surfaced; I have had odd comments made to me, betraying the speaker's assumptions about the nature of the process of recording.

On recording as "professional qualification"

Often, when people are asked what value ministers can have, the answers point to things like getting access to places (like prisons or hospitals), ecclesiastical endorsement of pastoral counsellors, having people who can speak or act officially (for example, perform weddings), and representation at things like clergy associations.

I must confess that I am very uneasy with the use of the process of recording of ministers to provide some kind of professional qualification. This uneasiness stems from several sources. The decline of gospel ministry as a concern has coincided with an increase in the value placed upon formal training for Friends leaders, and with the establishment of the workshop or "invited leader" model of the Public Friend. It seems to me that we should be jealous to preserve our ideal of the free gospel ministry, which includes the assertion that anyone may be called, learned or not. Further, the line of thinking that there are many kinds of ministry—true and evident, without doubt—has been extended to devalue or overshadow the vocal ministry, despite its enormous importance to the rise and health of the Society.

For these reasons, it seems better to find different, but appropriate, ways to provide the kinds of "ecclesiastical endorsement" that may be needed for professional practice in fields such as pastoral counselling, chaplaincy, and so on.

But what has it meant to me, to be a "recorded minister?"

- The first effect I felt was one of encouragement. Friends took the opportunity to tell me that they thought my service had been of value, and would continue to be. Recorded ministers and others who had exercised leadership in the yearly meeting spoke of their own experience, encouraged me to contact them, and teased me. I have taken this to heart, and tried when I can to do the same for others who have been recognized since then.

- It provided me a pretext on which to make contact with other ministers, both officially endorsed and otherwise, in other yearly meetings that I passed through. In some sense, I felt that the colleagueship was now unavoidable, and part of my service; and it felt valuable to have the explicit support of my meeting.

- It made me consider carefully what my gifts or calling might really be. Was it what was complimented, when Friends talked to me about the recording, or about this or that workshop or meeting visit? I began to explore this in more depth for myself, to apply a new level of skepticism about my assumptions about myself. This sense of increased care, and of increased commitment to faithfulness, started during the process of deliberation about my recording, during which I felt that something important (both exciting and frightening) was taking place, and I was caught up in something whose integrity I needed to uphold as well I possibly could. I became quieter. I exercise much stricter discernment in accepting invitations to lead workshops or visit meetings, and regulate my meeting calendar as carefully as I can, to keep my schedule open for unexpected concerns to visit meetings or individuals.

- It made me uncomfortable, because it is clear that there were many around me who in other times would have been recorded, but who were carrying on with their concerns without any such label—as I had done, before. One minister, well known in these parts also, told me that although he accepted the status at the insistence of his meeting, he had resolved that he would not let it change anything he did.

- It made me consider how to be accountable in my meeting. While it is widely said or written that a minister by being recorded enters into a kind of covenant with his or her meeting, in very many cases this does not take any concrete or visible form. Neither the minister nor the meeting is sure how to proceed. This has been my experience in all four of the meetings where my membership has been, since I was recorded in 1983. This has been one of the areas in which I have tried to encourage some experimentation, and have been eager to hear from others' experiences.

At about the time I was recorded, there were discussions within our yearly meeting about the whole practice of recording, and a survey was done of the New England ministers, asking them how they'd been recorded, what difference it had made, and how this related to their life as members of their meetings now. This forced me, new to the guild, to figure out what added value it might bring to have someone so labeled. It seemed clear from many of the answers that were given that the recording had conferred no value, except when it was for some specific service (a pastorate, or prison access, for example). This seems to me to be related to the lack of guidance and mutual encouragement to service that is the rule in these times.

To conclude

My conclusions about the institution of recording ministers now run something like this:

The assertion that "we are all ministers" is, while potentially true, too trivial to carry much weight in the discussion about whether the spiritual body has any specialized organs at all, or is just a uniform mass, apparently democratic. Further, a discussion of these questions is usually framed too narrowly.

What I want to say is a little more concrete. I believe that the unprogrammed tradition of the Religious Society of Friends is in a period of great weakness. We are hesitant about declaring our faith, hesitant about our allegiance to our spiritual community, contentious about verbal formulations, limited in our demographics. We have poor skills for spiritual nurture, a weak ability to overcome internal conflict, and limited resources for continued spiritual growth beyond the first stages. Our education and spiritual nurture are geared to enquirers, and undeveloped for children or long-time Friends.

In the past, the Society had a system within which these tasks were possible to do. The system includes the meetings for business, the meetings for worship, the meetings of ministers and elders, the weekly, monthly, and annual rhythms of our group life, and their mirrored images in our homes and in ourselves. I do not say it was perfect, but it was there, and Friends accepted that it should exist, and also that it should change as needed (though carefully).

Many of the issues confronting Friends have to do with spiritual authority, leadership, and the care of communities. The ministry—what kinds there are, how it should be supported, how it affects the community—is a central focus of all these issues. In working out answers to these questions, we also have to confront the whole question, central to Friends' experience, of the relationship between the individual and the community. How does the community exercise discernment? What influence should it exert on the members' lives? What do members owe the meeting?

The institution of the recorded ministry rested on several important assertions: that the community has a spiritual life that needs cultivation; that the cultivation needs specific attention, in parallel with care of the members individually; that God calls people to specific service, in varying degrees and for varying lengths of time, and in various kinds. How do we recognize, support, and shape concerns in a meeting? It must in the end focus on the Friend under concern—you cannot support for long "the ministry" without supporting the ministers—the carriers of the concern. Therefore, a recorded minister in these days in some sense incarnates the need to consider these questions as part of the life of the meeting, and the Religious Society of Friends at large. People are reluctant to get down to naming and working with particular people, so a recognized minister is an easy mark, since he or she has already been singled out, and thus can serve (in these experimental times) as a "guinea pig" for explorations in applied spirituality.

The guinea pig role is an important one, in my experience. I have sometimes felt that my service among Friends might be characterized by the recognition of a need, followed by a sense that others were not quite ready to take the first step, followed by my trying to do it, doing it inadequately, but opening the way for others to really get it right.

Finally, and more generally, the institution of recorded ministers has in the past supported collegiality among Friends experienced in following a certain kind of call over long periods of time, and has provided a kind of apprenticeship for Friends entering onto such a long-term calling. This is certainly not provided for by our current practice, either by clearness committees or by the meetings on ministry and counsel. This lack of cultivation over time means that our ministry tends to stay within rather narrow bounds, and we see little growth in the gifts, little grounded experimentation within the ministry of any one person that reflects some authentic spiritual progress.

The meeting always is most healthy when there is a variety of ministries being exercised, and some of the forms of ministry, including vocal ministry, or better gospel ministry, take time to "master." That is, after some time of following a call to visitation of the sick, or of visiting in families, you get better at it, if you are reflective about it, and have colleagues to consult with about how it went. Many ministries that require this kind of ripening are rarely or ever exercised now, because we don't feel capable.

This has more than antiquarian interest. I am not interested in reviving "meetings for apprentices" and the like just because once we had them. An important feature of our spiritual landscape in the past was the belief that worship might break out at any time, in any context, for any group. A Friend whose primary aim was watchfulness for such occasions could help make real the possibilities of the holy in any moment. Such a person on the alert can inject a sense of presence and reverence into any gathering. This enables the group to be creative in its sense of the sacred, helps it develop more ways to hallow all aspect of life.

A critical outgrowth of this sense of identification with others who shared the work was that part of a minister's call was always and everywhere to be sensitive to "the springs of life breaking forth in any" (to quote Fox). Ministers were to call out the gifts of others, and lovingly encourage them in faithfulness.

Finally, I think that recognized ministers (and anyone bearing a minute for service or travel) are part of a pact with their meetings, and should be willing both to submit their leadings to the meeting's discernment, and to listen when Friends suggest ways of service that might be appropriate to consider. All ministry should come with a sense of fresh requirement by God, but one can never tell how a call might come. A call from the meeting may well be in right ordering. Such a relationship is to the meeting's benefit as well.

Our yearly meeting has often discussed how to encourage appropriate care of ministers, and has asked meetings to consider this, but I am not aware of any progress yet towards clear guidance. Some Friends have a support committee, though I think ministry and counsel (and other elders) should be the location for such contacts and nurture. I do think that the minister has a responsibility for reporting to ministry and counsel on some regular basis. In my own experience, writing such a report to the meeting as a whole has been one way to help us all learn about accountability; and I have found that the series of reports is a very useful aid in my own reflection about my work. In writing this report every year, I make sure that I identify specific areas of work that seem to be in prospect, so that Friends can ask questions if they wish. I also make a point of reporting on what happened on those points from last year. I try honestly to sit with the possibility that the concern has left me, and if not, I feel the need to try to state the concern clearly as part of the report, just as anyone seeking a travel minute for other kinds of work is expected to do. There should be no assumptions of privilege, and no coasting.

Friends who feel a calling must see it as their right and duty to seek to ground it within their community, for confirmation, guidance, stimulation, and discipline. The community should somehow include the monthly meeting. This might seem to go without saying, but in fact we often must seek outside our meetings for guidance and support, especially at times of tenderness or new growth. A meeting rarely can provide the all-sufficient nourishment for its members. Yet ministry must be grounded in truth, and that includes the truth of our local meeting. This will sometimes be uncomfortable and awkward, and the shape it takes can remain elusive for years. The only way to persist is to remain in a teachable spirit, and to give the highest priority to a reverent care and stewardship of a real concern or calling.

To summarize

I do not claim that the old machinery is what we need, but that the old machinery was (1) consistent with our theology, and (2) addressed real needs which are not now being met. Since few of us grew up in a setting where the old traditions lived on in some measure, the old ways cannot mean the same to us now. But they can be instructive and challenging. This includes the ways in which the traditional practices were not adequate to their tasks, of course—no social system is perfect! Our challenge as a Society is to face the real needs of our community. What will release and make the best use of our gifts and opportunities? The discussion of recording must continue among us in such a way that we do not just reach some conclusions about an old custom, but we take creative steps that build both our current understanding, and on three centuries of Quaker practice—practice in a very specific spiritual path with its own boundaries and its own kinds of truth.

Another way to put this is: One way to describe the "meaning" of a group, like our Religious Society of Friends, is that it seeks to fully embody the vision given it. I believe that we perhaps have focused too much on belief, and too little on practices of faithfulness which are based on a real, challenging encounter with the spirit of Christ. In the past, when Friends had looked so uniform, do you think they all *thought* the same? The glimpses we have of private thoughts and beliefs suggest that within the orthodox demeanor there were often quite heterodox thoughts and meanings. This is OK with me, as I think about it now. It seems to me a more fruitful approach to combating the swift erosion of our Society's meaning to consider whether we can agree, meeting by meeting, on how a Friend should act and live, rather than how he or she should believe. Practices are not merely external, are not merely "form," but can provide a vessel into which meaning is poured—and transformed—if the encounter with the Other is real, and we are not just communing with ourselves.

A body of Friends, whose avowed task is to maintain inward and outward spiritual watchfulness, and to sometimes articulate (in the right times and the right places) what they see, in warning, questioning, guidance, or encouragement, may well serve our community powerfully as we reach towards faithfulness—seeing and seeking the lawfulness that is at the heart of gospel freedom, and making it truthfully part of our every day.

APPENDIX 2

Sample annual reports to monthly meeting

1 Twelfth Month 2003

Dear Friends:

When I was at Lynn Meeting, I had the custom of writing a short account each year of the things I had done under a sense of duty as a recorded minister. I was not in the position of a pastor there, and ministry and counsel hardly met; I had no appointed oversight. Yet I was convinced (as I still am) that we should take seriously the duty to ensure that ministers are faithful in their gift, and also that they take note if the concern is to be laid down. The meeting on ministry and counsel might inquire about this, but the minister ought also to be ready to reflect aloud, as part of his or her discipline with the meeting. I didn't do this at Fresh Pond, because it might have caused more trouble than it was worth. As our meeting is gaining strength, and is comfortable with the practice of recording, it seems to me a good thing to take up again.

Before I start, I should say a couple of things.

1. [Another minister in the meeting] may not wish to follow this practice, and I would be quite comfortable if that is her feeling. I am not aware of any other minister in the yearly meeting who does this kind of thing; as far as I know it's an invention of my own. I feel the concern to do it, and to recommend it, but that's all.

2. I am not requesting any particular response from the meeting, but would be glad to hear comment, critique, etc. in any form, private or public—either on the report itself, or what ought to be in such a report.

In what follows, I will try to state my concern briefly, the forms of action it seems to take, then describe what I've done under this concern, and finally how the coming year looks.

A. My concern

My concern is for gospel ministry. What I mean by this is, to speak or write as I am led, to support and encourage Friends as they seek to grow in the knowledge of God, and in imaginative, fervent, open, humble, and joyous obedience to the motions of the divine life in them and their Friends.

Because of this concern, I want Friends to take advantage of the great wealth of wisdom and insight that resides in the Quaker tradition—I want them to become "masters of the Quaker way." This means helping people see what resources there are in the Quaker experience (as well as in the wider Christian world and the scriptures) and to see how to make profitable use of these resources in their own lives.

To do this, and to be fit to do it as well as possible, I feel that I make good use of my talents and experience in working to interpret Quakerism from across the centuries to modern Friends; this means study. Further, I need to work as hard as possible on my own faithfulness and spiritual practice, and to reflect upon my experience, so as to put it at the service of others, for what it's worth. Finally, I need to take all this and put it to work, and that means writing, teaching, and preaching as way opens.

In all this, I have a special concern for any Friends who are under concern, especially those who are coming into the ministry, because I believe that modern Friends are not very skilled at living with a long-term concern for the ministry, nor at supporting such people to be as faithful and diligent in their gift as possible.

B. The past year

Last year the meeting gave me a travel minute to visit among New England Friends, especially to meet with those who are active in vocal ministry. Under this minute so far, I have visited Burlington, Durham, and Hartford (twice), and led a retreat for Storrs Meeting on the general topic of vocal ministry. I also led a forum at Concord Meeting last month, on the peace testimony. I have contacted a few other meetings for opportunities with them, and expect that I will be visiting several meetings in the next few months. My hope in general is to visit at least one meeting a month.

Formal engagements. However, I get a steady trickle of invitations to do other things. My practice is to sit in prayer with each one as it comes, and feel whether there is a stop in my mind about doing it. If not, then I try to see how it relates to my concern, so that I don't dissipate my energies and limited time. Then, when I accept the invitation, I know that my concern will find its place in that context. My general practice is to limit engagements that take much preparation to three per year. I have found it increasingly easy to say "No" to things which might otherwise be very exciting to do (for example, *Faith and Practice* revision, or being a speaker at another yearly meeting), and each time I have done so, I have felt affirmation that in this, at least, I was being faithful.

This year, I have accepted three such invitations. First, I was a resource person for the School of the Spirit, and led two sessions on Gospel Order at their residency in September. This was a great opportunity for me, as I was led to consider very deeply what the nature of Gospel Order is, both historically and as experienced, and also to think about where we need to be spiritually so that we can be "ordered." It also clarified for me how important it is that in this century Friends under concern really learn from the exercise of their calling, and use it to challenge and extend their own spiritual lives and practice in an intentional way.

Second, I gave a session on "Meeting for Worship through History," for the Salem Quarterly Meeting Quaker Studies Program. This led me to consider more carefully in my own mind how to make the threads of continuity throughout Quaker history as accessible as possible, while also showing how different we have been from century to century. It also led me to a fresh statement of the gospel as Friends hold it, as a challenge to us modern Friends.

Finally, I co-led a retreat at Woolman Hill (along with Bill How from Fresh Pond) called "How do we inhabit our time?"

which was a workshop for Friends to grapple with their uses of time, and their sense that they never have enough time, or don't use their time well. This also turned out to be an important learning session for me, and has made a difference both in my own practice, and in my understanding of Christian life; these fresh lessons in turn are good resources for any future service I may perform.

Writing. I have felt this past year that it is time for me to be writing more. I have several pieces that I hope to complete in the next couple of months. The major benefit I can see from this, aside from any value of the writings themselves, is that in order to do this, I will need to be disciplined about writing regularly, and with real attention to craft and revision—and therefore I will have done the difficult things I will have to do to claim the time and space I need, and then use them faithfully!

The pieces I can see right now, which I have done at least initial work on, are:

- with Gordon Bugbee, a piece on James Nayler's thought;
- a Pendle Hill Pamphlet on Nayler's message;
- three columns for the *Friends Journal* on Nayler, Steere, and Margaret Fell;
- a book of counsel and comfort for Friends in the ministry, a sort of modern response to Samuel Bownas's useful book from 1750.

All these are in part preparation for a larger work on early Quaker spirituality which I have had in mind for a long time, and which I hope to spend much of the next 5 or 6 years on, if way opens. The goal is not antiquarian, but to help modern Friends understand just how broad and ambitious Quaker spirituality can be—to provide some support or encouragement to the many good Friends who are feeling the trends, pressures, griefs, and confusions of the time, and yet also are feeling the Lord at work.

Other. I believe that because of my concern, I need to be open to various other tasks that may come my way—clearness committees, oversight committees, correspondence, etc. I am at present on M's oversight committee, and one for a certain Friend (for her concern for Cuba); I am also an "Oversight and discernment" member for Puente de Amigos. I have tried to be more faithful in attending yearly meeting ministry and counsel this year, and this will require continuing effort to manage the calendar.

C. Next year.

First, I should say that my sense of calling, and desire for more diligent and responsive service, continues with me. The following are commitments I am making, God willing, upon which I will reflect around this time next year:

1. I hope to be able to report on other meeting visits under my travel minute; I do not feel that concern has been laid down, and there is much yet to do.

2. I hope to have completed the writing projects listed above, and seen my way to the next round of work of this type.

3. I note that I have felt an occasional pull to hold public meetings for worship among nonFriends. This is not yet on my plate, but I note that it has recurred several times in the past year, and I wonder if this will go away, or become stronger.

4. I intend to continue attending the majority of yearly meeting ministry and counsel meetings.

5. My personal practice currently includes daily retirement, prayer, and scripture reading (for at least a few minutes), and as often as possible writing in my journal. I also find it important to read the journals of Friends ministers from the past, as a way to keep my sense of apprenticeship in the school of Christ. I hope that I can continue this general pattern, and deepen both my prayer and my encounter with scripture, which I have found myself reading in a new and fresh way these past few months.

6. I do not have a regular support committee, and I do not feel the need to request one. I do have several Friends to whom I feel accountable, and I hope during this year to be a little bolder in talking with them about my own work.

Report from the following year

12 First Month 2004

Dear Friends:

As I wrote last year, I here report on my service in the ministry over the past year. I believe that recorded ministers, like any other Friend whose service has been encouraged by the meeting, are under obligation to stay in dialogue with the meeting about their service. While the minister must first consult God in considering what to do, he or she is also responsible to the meeting, and should be willing and indeed eager for guidance and advice. As always, I will be grateful for comments on this report, or requests for clarification, etc.

A. My concern is for gospel ministry

What I mean by this is, to speak or write as I am led, to support and encourage Friends as they seek to grow in the knowledge of God, and in imaginative, fervent, open, humble, and joyous obedience to the motions of the divine life in them and their Friends.

To do this, and to be fit to do it as well as possible, I feel that I make good use of my talents and experience in working to interpret Quakerism from across the centuries to modern Friends; this means fairly constant study. Further, I need to work as hard as possible on my own faithfulness and spiritual practice, and to reflect upon my experience, so as to put it at the service of others, for what it's worth. Finally, I need to take all this and put it to work, and that means writing, listening, teaching, and preaching as way opens. It means setting aside any opportunities or invitations that do not seem to support this work, or might supplant it somehow; I believe I have been fairly careful in making these choices. As I said last year, my main desire now is to be as diligent and available as possible to opportunities for service.

This past fall marked the twentieth year since Salem Quarter recorded my gift in the ministry. I have never found this to be anything but a stimulant (or even a goad) to service, and I believe that I have in fact grown in my willingness and ability to respond to specific opportunities that might come my way. As I wrote last year, I have a special concern for any Friends who are under concern, especially those who are coming into the ministry, because I believe that modern Friends are not very skilled at living with a long-term concern for the ministry, nor at supporting such people to be as faithful and diligent in their gift as possible. I believe that I have been serviceable, and more diligent, in this kind of "ministry to ministers" over the past year.

It is important that anyone with a long-term concern be open to considering whether the concern continues, or should be laid down. I believe that my concern continues, or, to put it another way, I feel a real sense of demand and urgency to continue in the work.

B. *The past year*

Meeting visits. I have notes on visits under concern to the following, this past year: Worcester, Concord (3 times), Dover (3 times), Concord Meeting on Ministry and Counsel, Dover Meeting on Ministry and Counsel. Since last fall, when the meeting received back my travel minute, and liberated me for visitation once a month, I have tried to find other opportunities to get to know meetings, beyond the regular Sunday meetings; the monthly meetings on ministry and counsel have seemed to provide an interesting opportunity, which I will continue to seek as I move ahead with travel this year. I believe that steady work in this regard will open the way for other kinds of service. In that connection, I have been more diligent in seeking opportunities with individuals with a concern for the ministry; these opportunities (perhaps eight of them in the past few months) provide a time of prayer and conversation which are refreshing to both visitor and visited. After each meeting visit or opportunity, I take time to write reflectively about it, so that I have a record of things noted at the meetings there, as well as events that I found personally instructive, people I should stay in contact with, etc.

In a special category is the trip to Kenya. As with my trip to Cuba, I went to Kenya primarily to accompany and support another Friend's ministry, in this case Darcy as she followed her concern there. This was an important time for me, however, as it was instructive and challenging to my faith and understanding of the role of Friends in the world, and required that I work to articulate the importance and value of traditional Quaker spirituality among Kenyan Friends. An interesting opening was the address I gave at the Friends Theological Institute. I was able also in a small way to encourage some Friends in the ministry.

I am now clear to undertake one or two public meetings for worship for nonFriends this year, a concern I mentioned in my last report, and in speaking to the meeting this fall. I am exploring how to proceed with this idea, with Jonathan Vogel-Borne, who wishes to join me.

Formal engagements. Last year, I had only two formal tasks, both at yearly meeting: participation in the panel on conflict, and offering one of the Bible half hours.

Writing. I have undertaken quite a lot of writing this past year (in addition to a fairly large correspondence), and accomplished pretty much what I had hoped to when writing my last report. In addition to several review essays in Friends Journal, I wrote the first two articles on "Quaker Writings," to be part of a regular feature in *Friends Journal.* These two were on Nayler and Steere, and will be followed this year by two more on Margaret Fell and Mary Penington.

I have begun writing the book of advice and counsel for Friends in the ministry that I've long had in view, and hope to have a complete draft of that by Fifth Month.

I have arranged for a team consisting of myself, Hugh Barbour, and Gordon Bugbee to write a review article for *Quaker Religious Thought* on a new edition of Nayler's works; getting this done is an executive as much as an intellectual task, as the three of us are hard to collect!

Further writing on Nayler has ceased for the time being, as it became clear that Pendle Hill was in a period of turmoil about their editorial direction, and so correspondence about that project just stopped for some months.

Other. I believe that because of my concern, I need to be open to various other tasks that may come my way—clearness committees, oversight committees, correspondence, etc. I am at present on Marian's oversight committee, and one for Susan Furry (for her concern for Cuba); I am also an "Oversight and discernment" member for Puente de Amigos. Other groups I have been part of: I have attended the East African Interest Group, in support of Darcy; and I have been an instigator of the Quaker Peacebuilder Camp project that is currently in development, spearheaded by John Humphries of Hartford Meeting. I have managed to be more faithful in attending yearly meeting ministry and counsel this year, and was able to play a significant role in the writing of the yearly meeting's State of Society report.

C. Next year

The following are commitments I am making, God willing, upon which I will reflect around this time next year:

1. I hope to be able to report on other meeting visits.

2. I hope to have completed the writing projects listed above, and seen my way to the next round of work of this type.

3. I will hold a few public meetings for nonFriends—it is not clear how many, but when I undertake them I will report to the meeting.

4. I intend to continue attending the majority of yearly meeting ministry and counsel meetings.

5. Events: I have the three commitments I try to limit myself to all lined up: (a) The first weekend in March I will be leading a workshop at Woolman Hill (with Maggie Edmondson) entitled "Minding the light." (b) I will make a presentation as part of a week-long workshop at the FGC Gathering this summer: my subject is Job Scott, an interesting New England Friend of the eighteenth century. (c) At FGC, and probably at yearly meeting, I will participate in an evening with Rex Ambler, exploring before an audience some comparisons between Fox's and Nayler's understanding of the Quaker path.

6. My personal practice currently includes daily retirement, prayer, and scripture reading (for at least a few minutes), and as often as possible writing in my journal. I also find it important to read the journals of Friends ministers from the past, as a way to keep my sense of apprenticeship in the school of Christ. This past year, along with Darcy Drayton, I have joined in the Spiritual Formation program that yearly meeting ministry and counsel members are doing together. In addition, I believe I should take more opportunities to get together concerned Friends from other meetings, so will probably attend a couple of retreats as I did in Barnesville last fall.

A bibliography on Quaker ministry and other works cited

Abbreviations for commonly cited periodicals:

FQE   *Friends Quarterly Examiner*

FJ   *Friends Journal*

FQ   *Friends Quarterly*

QRT   *Quaker Religious Thought*

NOTE: Many citations from journals provide only the first page of the article. Note also that the high proportion of citations from *FQE* results from an intensive search for discussion about the practice of recording, and its relation to cultivation of gifts, in London Yearly Meeting.

** Marks works especially of interest. In addition, the journals of Hoag, Scott, Bownas, and Woolman are very instructive.

**Abbott, Margery Post and Peggy Senger Parsons, eds. 2004. *Walk worthy of your calling: Quakers and the travelling ministry.* Richmond, IN: Friends United Press.

Albright, M. Catherine. 1914. The cultivation of the gift of ministry. *FQE* 48:359.

Atack, Benjamin. 1898. The ministry of the word. *FQE* 32:562.

Barbour, Hugh. 1964. *The Quakers in Puritan England.* New Haven: Yale University Press.

Barclay, Robert. 2002 [1678]. *An apology for the true Christian divinity.* Glendale, PA: Quaker Heritage Press, and Warminster, PA: Peter D. Sippel.

Bauman, Richard. 1983. *Let your words be few: Symbolism of speaking and silence among seventeenth-century Quakers.* Cambridge: Cambridge University Press.

Beamish, Lucia K. 1963. Consecrated ministry. *FQ* 14(8):343–52.

Beamish, Lucia K. 1967. *Quaker ministry 1691 to 1834*. Privately published.

**Benson, Lewis. 1979. On being moved by the Spirit to minister in public worship. *New Foundation Publications* no. 4, pp.48–51. Gloucester, England: George Fox Fund.

**Bownas, Samuel. 1989. *A description of the qualifications necessary to a gospel minister.* Wallingford, PA: Pendle Hill Publications.

Bownas, Samuel. 1839. *An account of the life, travels, and Christian experiences of Samuel Bownas, a minister of the Gospel in the Society of Friends.* In W. Evans and T. Evans (eds.) Friends Library, 3:1–70. Philadelphia: Printed by Joseph Rakestraw, for the editors.

Braithwaite, W.C. 1921. The recording of ministers. *FQE* 55(3) pg. 297.

Brayshaw, A. Neave. 1914. The problem of the free ministry. *FQE* 48:359.

Brayshaw, A. Neave. 1969 [1953]. *The Quakers: their story and message.* London: Friends Home Service Committee.

Brinton, Howard H. date unknown. *Prophetic ministry.* Pendle Hill Pamphlet #54. Wallingford, PA: Pendle Hill.

Brinton, Howard H. 1960. Friends for seventy-five years. *The Bulletin of the Friends Historical Association* 49(1):3–20.

Brinton, Howard H. 1974. *Quaker Journals: varieties of religious experience in the Religious Society of Friends.* Wallingford, PA: Pendle Hill Publications.

Budge, Francis. 1882. Samuel Bownas. *FQE* 16:561.

Burnyeat, John. 1691. *The Truth exalted in the writings of that eminent and faithful servant of Christ, John Burnyeat.* London: Thomas Northcott.

Capper, Mary. 1860. *A memoir of Mary Capper, lately of Birmingham, a minister of the Society of Friends.* Philadelphia: Association of Friends for the dissemination of religious and useful knowledge.

Chase, Thomas. 1882. Consecrated scholarship in the Society of Friends. *FQE* 16:386.

Comfort, Howard. 1959. Concerning worship and ministry—Part I. *FJ* Jan. 24:52–3

Comfort, Howard. 1959. Concerning worship and ministry—Part II. *FJ* Feb. 7:84–5.

Conran, John. 1877. *A journal of the life and Gospel labours of John Conran.* Philadelphia: Henry Longstreth.

Crisp, Stephen. 1850 [1894]. *The Christian experiences, Gospel labours and writings of that ancient servant of Christ, Stephen Crisp.* Philadelphia: The Friends' Library 14:134–278.

Dale, Jonathan. 1996. *Beyond the spirit of the age: Quaker social responsibility at the end of the twentieth century.* London: Quaker Home Service.

Dennis, E.T.W. 1913. Family Worship. *FQE* 47:76.

**Doncaster, Phoebe. 1908. *John Stephenson Rowntree: his life and work.* London: Headley Brothers.

Drayton, Brian. 1988. Notes on the Friends practice called "recording gifts in the ministry." Unpublished ditto.

Drayton, Brian. 1994. *Selections from the writings of James Nayler.* 2nd ed. Worcester, MA: Mosher Book and Tract Fund of New England Yearly Meeting.

Drayton, Brian. 1996. *Treasure in earthen vessels.* Worcester, MA: Mosher Book and Tract Fund of New England Yearly Meeting.

Drayton, Brian. 1997. Being a recorded minister. Published by Pendle Hill, at http://www.pendlehill.org/newpage11.htm

Drayton, Brian. 2004. Darwin's journals—and yours. *Hands On!* 27(1):18–20.

Dymond, Joseph John. 1892. *Gospel Ministry in the Society of Friends: A series of letters.* London: Edward Hicks, Jun.

Dymond, Joseph John. 1897. The recording of ministers. *FQE* 31: 155.

Ellis, Ellen M. 1882. On the need of preparing ourselves for our work. *FQE* 16:356.

Erskine, Ruth. 1910. Quaker ministry. *FQE* 44:465.

Forbush, Bliss. 1956. *Elias Hicks: Quaker liberal.* New York: Columbia University Press.

Forbush, Bliss. 1985. On the recording of ministers. *FJ* Sept. 1:5–6.

Fox, George. *Journal.* See Nickalls, John L. 1952.

Fox, Rachel. 1897. The recording of ministers. *FQE* 31:57.

Fry, Joan Mary. 1913. Eldership from the point of view of the ministry. *FQE* 47:374.

Gillett, George. 1880. Gospel Preaching. *FQE* 14:434.

**Glover, Sue. 1997. *Go and the Lord go with thee!* York: Sessions Book Trust.

Graham, John W. 1904. An analysis of ministry. *FQE* 38:209.

Graham, John W. 1929. *The Faith of a Quaker,* ch. IV–VI. London: PUBLISHER?

Graham, John W. 1933. *Psychical experiences of Quaker ministers.* London: Friends Historical Society.

**Graham, John W. 1925. *The Quaker ministry.* Swarthmore Lecture, 1925. London: The Swarthmore Press Ltd.

Griffith, John. 1779. *Journal of John Griffith.* London.

Grubb, Edward. 1888. On the ministry in our meetings. *FQE* 21:366.

Grubb, Edward. 1907. Use of the Old Testament in Preaching. *FQE* 41:173.

Grubb, Sarah Lynes (1863) *A brief account of the life and religious labors of Sarah Grubb.* Philadelphia: The Tract Association of Friends.

**Grundy, Martha Paxson, ed. 2001. *Resistance and obedience to God: memoirs of David Ferris.* Philadelphia: Quaker Press of Friends General Conference.

**Grundy, Martha Paxson. 1999. *Tall poppies: supporting gifts of ministry and eldering in the monthly meeting.* Wallingford, PA: Pendle Hill Publications. Pendle Hill Pamphlet #347.

Gummere, Amelia Mott. 1901. *The Quaker: a study in costume.* Philadelphia: Ferris & Leach Publishers.

Harris, Henry. 1912. Thoughts on eldership. *FQE* 46:317.

**Harvey, T. Edmund. 1946. Our Quaker ministry since the cessation of recording. *FQE* 80:187–92.

**Hibbert, G. K. 1933. *A plea for a deeper ministry.* London: Friends' Book Centre.

Hicks, Edward. 1851. *Memoirs of the life and religious labors of Edward Hicks.* Written by himself. Philadelphia: Merrihew & Thompson, Printers.

Hoag, Joseph. 1861. *Journal of the life of Joseph Hoag, an eminent minister of the Gospel in the Society of Friends.* Auburn, NY: Knapp and Peck, Printers.

Jeavons, Thomas. 1984. Living ministry. *Friends General Conference Quarterly* 16(2):1ff.

Jenkins, James. 1984. *The Records and recollections of James Jenkins.* Edited by J. William Frost. Texts and Studies in Religion, Vol. 18. New York: The Edwin Mellen Press.

Jones, Ernest. 1912. The threshing meeting. *FQE* 46:463.

Moulton, Phillips P. 1971. *The Journal and major essays of John Woolman.* New York: Oxford University Press.

Naish, C.G. 1922. Habitual speakers in Friends' Meetings. *FQE* 56(2):10.

Nayler, James. 2004. *The Works of James Nayler.* Vol. 2. Glenside, PA: Quaker Heritage Press.

Newman, Henry S. 1886. Gospel ministry. *FQE* 20:526–37.

Nickalls, John L., ed. 1952. *The Journal of George Fox.* Cambridge: at the University Press.

North Carolina Yearly Meeting (Conservative). 2000. Vocal Ministry. *Journal of the North Carolina Yearly Meeting (Conservative)* Vol. 1.

Nuttall, Geoffrey F. 1967. The minister's devotional life. In *The Puritan Spirit*. London: The Epworth Press. 246–54.

**Nuttall, Geoffrey F. 1959. *To the refreshing of the Children of Light*. Pendle Hill Pamphlet #101. Wallingford, PA: Pendle Hill.

Penington, Isaac. 1995–7. *The works of Isaac Penington, a minister of the Gospel in the Society of Friends*. Glenside, PA: Quaker Heritage Press. Vols. 1 to 4.

**Penn, William. 1980. *The rise and progress of the people called Quakers*. Reprint edition. Richmond, IN: Friends United Press.

Pollard, F. E. 1898. The training of the will. *FQE* 32: 223.

Pollard, William. 1881. The Christian ministry. *FQE* 15: 28.

Pollard, William. 1881. Our small meetings. *FQE* 15:447.

Punshon, John. 1982. *Alternative Christianity*. Walllingford, PA: Pendle Hill Publications: Pendle Hill Pamphlet #245.

Richardson, Jane M. 1882. Early Friends as evangelists. *FQE* 16: 236.

Robson, Isaac. 1882. Christian ministry. *FQE* 16: 17

Rowntree, John S. 1904. Gospel Ministry in the Society of Friends. *FQE* pp. 415–36.

Rowntree, John S. 1896. Meetings on Ministry and Oversight. I. *FQE* 30:441.

Rowntree, John S. 1897. Meetings on Ministry and Oversight. II. *FQE* 31:248.

Rowntree, Joshua. 1897. The recording of ministers. *FQE* 31: 63.

Scott, Job. 1993. *Essays on Salvation by Christ and the debate which followed their publication*. Glenside, PA: Quaker Heritage Press.

**Scott, Job. 1831. *The works of that eminent minister of the Gospel, Job Scott, late of Providence, Rhode Island*. Two vols. Philadelphia: John Comly.

Sessions, Frederick. 1897. The preacher's preparation for his work. *FQE* 31:11.

Sharp, Isaac, Jr. 1887. Christian ministry. *FQE* 21:522–36.

Skidmore, Gil. 2003. *Strength in weakness: writings by eighteenth-century Quaker women.* Oxford: Rowman & Littlefield Publishers, Inc.

Snell, Beatrice Saxon. 1980. The ministry of speech. *The Friend* July 11:861–62.

**Steere. Douglas. 1955. *On listening to another.* New York: Harper and Row.

Sturge, Matilda. 1882. An old-fashioned sermon. *FQE* 16:87.

**Taber, William P. 1980. The theology of the inward imperative: travelling Quaker ministry of the middle period. *QRT* 18(4): 3–19.

Taber, William P. 1985. *The Eye of Faith: A history of Ohio Yearly Meeting, Conservative.* Barnesville, OH: Ohio Yearly Meeting of Friends.

**Taber, William P. 1996. Quaker ministry: the inward motion and the razor's edge. http://www.quaker.org/pendle-hill/taber.html.

Tallack, William. 1889. Personal and ministerial responsibility, with special reference to small meetings. *FQE* 23:585.

Thomas, A. L. 1919. J. *Bevan Braithwaite: A Friend of the XIX Century.* London: Hodder.

Warner, E. 1904. Ministry from the objective standpoint. *FQE* 38:224

Warner, E. 1904. The problem before our Yearly Meeting: the ministry in our meetings. 3 parts, *FQE.* 89ff.

West, Jessamyn. 1990. *The Quaker reader.* Wallingford, PA: Pendle Hill Publications.

Wilson, Lloyd Lee. 2000. Accountability and vocal ministry. *Journal of the North Carolina Yearly Meeting (Conservative)* 1:8–11.

**Wilson, Lloyd Lee. 1993. *Essays on the Quaker vision of Gospel Order.* Philadelphia, PA: Quaker Press of Friends General Conference.

**Wilson, Lloyd Lee. 2000. Vocal ministry of one Friend. *Journal of the North Carolina Yearly Meeting (Conservative)* 1:6–8.

**Wilson, Lloyd Lee. 2005. *Wrestling with Our Faith Tradition: Collected Public Witness, 1995–2004.* Philadelphia, PA: Quaker Press of Friends General Conference.

Woolman, John. *Journal and major essays.* See Moulton, Phillips P. 1971.